All That is Seen and Unseen

See all there is to see!

—Elizabeth Peterson

All That is Seen and Unseen

A Journey Through a First Trimester Miscarriage

Elizabeth Petrucelli

A MEMOIR

Dragonfly Press, LLC
Parker, CO

Published by Dragonfly Press, LLC

Library of Congress Control Number: 2012932761
ISBN: 978-0-9851713-0-8
ISBN: 978-0-9851713-1-5 (eBook)

Edited by Shadia Duske – psychotherapy-healing.com & Melanie Saxton - melaniesaxtononline.com
Cover Design by Ted Ruybal – bluetailbooks.com
Cover Image © 2012 by Joanne Eberstein (Elizabeth's mother)

This book is nonfiction and based on a true life event. Some names have been change to protect their identities.

DISCLAIMER:

This book's aim is to serve as a guide for women. It is not intended to serve as medical advice. The author accepts no liability or responsibility for any loss or damage caused or thought to be caused by following the advice in this book and recommends that you consult a healthcare professional for medical advice or questions you may have with the advice contained herein.

Visit this book's website at www.allthatisseenandunseen.com.

To the daughter I will never hold
Ruby Josephine

Acknowledgements

For my husband Jason, thank you for being my "rock" and "knight in shining armor." You are an amazing husband and father. Thank you for being patient with me while compiling this book.

For my son Joseph, whom I adore. Thank you for your patience and support while I spent many nights with the door closed in the second bedroom and for your tiny knocks to tell me good night.

For my original editor, who also happens to be my therapist. Without your skills, I would have never grown from this experience. Thank you for pushing me to reach deep inside my soul and for helping me to express myself in ways I never thought possible.

For all my friends who gave me loving support throughout this loss, especially Tiffany and Glenna.

And finally, I want to thank my parents for helping me to grow into the person that I am today.

I hope this book will help you see that you are not alone. Your loss will be different than the next woman's loss, but I hope that reading my story will help you work through your loss and allow you to know that it's normal to feel the emotions you are feeling. First trimester loss can be just as devastating as a loss at any gestational period. I want people to understand that this grief is real and women experiencing an early loss deserve to grieve. We have nothing to be ashamed of.

A person is a person, no matter how small.

– Doctor Seuss

NOTE: This book contains journal entries which may contain grammatical errors due to the author's desire to preserve the journal entries in their most raw form.

All That is Seen and Unseen
A Journey Through a First Trimester Miscarriage

Chapter 1

It's been a little over a week since I learned I was pregnant with you. I don't know who you are or if you will stay with me, but the last week has been very stressful and I want to write down my thoughts for you. You see, I was set to have surgery next week to repair my ACL I tore while testing for a local police department. Now that you are growing inside me, I am unable to have the surgery.

When I first learned I was pregnant with you on St. Patrick's Day 2010, a wide range of emotions filled me. At first I was shocked. I realized that all that I had been working for over the last year would once again be put on hold. With surgery pending, I would be in limbo again. I had a small window of opportunity to complete the journey of becoming a police officer. After about 30 minutes, I began to cry. No, I wasn't exactly happy. I felt my life was over and I was going to have to start all over again. While we had been praying for a baby for years, it seemed this was the wrong time.

I was born in New York and raised in Tulsa, Oklahoma due to a job transfer my dad experienced. My parents were native New Yorkers and left both their families behind to start a new life in Oklahoma. My mother gave birth to four children, three girls and a boy. My brother was child number two. I'm number three and shared a room with my younger sister for fifteen years.

As a young child I enjoyed things most kids did — climbing trees, riding my bike, and spending time with friends. As a teenager I did well in school and was a dedicated member of my high school band and FFA chapter. I was an attractive young girl with long blonde hair, green eyes, and an athletic build. I had my share of boyfriends but wasn't sexually active. My desire was to get married in my early 20's and have my first child by the time I was 23.

My menstrual cycle didn't start until I was 15 and I only had one or two periods a year. When I did have a period it would last 15 days. I wasn't able to go to school due to the pain and copious amounts of blood. At the time, I didn't realize this was a problem. I thought this was how all girls had their periods. My mom got me birth control when I was 17 to regulate my menstrual cycle. I began to have periods every 30 days, and since I didn't know much about fertility I never suspected I would have a problem conceiving.

I left home immediately after graduating from high school due to an ultimatum from my parents. They wanted me to stop dating the 27-year-old man I had been seeing for over a year. He refused to marry me several months after I moved in, and I left him. I moved back in with my parents and then joined the United States Marine Corps. I felt I needed a change and some good discipline.

I met my husband, Jason, while serving in the Marine Corps. We had both joined to serve as musicians. Unfortunately, I was severely injured in boot camp. Although I spent a year in recovery, I still wasn't quite healed enough to attend the School of Music. Instead, I was transferred to the base band for on-the-job training. I met my husband the day I was transferred to the band.

He introduced himself to me in the hallway as I was receiving my first tour of the building and gave me his barracks room and phone number. He was equipped like most Marines, outfitted in a dress uniform that would make any young woman's heart flutter. He had turquoise eyes and short brown hair in the typical "high and tight" style. He stood as tall as I but was quite skinny; the proverbial "wet cat." He was very attractive, but I was uncomfortable with his assertiveness and, quite frankly, felt that he was intrusive. I was turned off by this and swore I would stay away from him.

He persisted, despite my attempts to ignore his invitations to "stop by his room." In an effort to shut him down once and for all, I visited him and several of his friends one evening. Following the movie night in his room, Jason secretly left a note on my truck. His approach was romantic. The small note, folded into the rubber matting of my truck window, said, *Dinner, Friday Night, Best Italian Food in Town! - Jason.* Unfortunately, I read this in front of another Marine suitor. I only knew Jason by his last name, so when I read the note aloud my Marine suitor was distraught by Jason's forwardness. I was quite embarrassed.

My first date with Jason, however, was amazing. This date, coupled with match-making skills from Jason's friend Charley, brought us together and a year later we were married.

I stopped taking birth control pills shortly after because I thought they were making me fat. We were open to a child, but we weren't actively trying to get pregnant. We completed our tours of four years and then moved back to his home town of Aurora, Colorado. Colorado seemed like a better place to raise children because there were so many opportunities. I also enjoyed snow — something I didn't see much of in Oklahoma. I wanted my children to experience the joys snow can bring, the variety of seasons, and the awe of the mountains.

I didn't have a period for a whole year and decided to see a doctor. He diagnosed me with Polycystic Ovarian Syndrome and told me I needed to take birth control to lower my risk of ovarian cancer. The diagnosis meant that I didn't ovulate regularly, if at all. All my eggs would partially grow, getting stuck on my ovary and then leaving a cyst. It wasn't a favorable diagnosis for having children, but I had heard many women could overcome the challenges and conceive. After the diagnosis, we started trying to have a baby. I was put on some fertility drugs, but after seven months with no ovulation I had to stop. September 11, 2001 happened and we decided we wanted a family. It was time to get serious about it.

Jason got tested, and I had more tests done. Jason's tests came back perfect. I was referred to an infertility specialist and took another six months worth of fertility drugs with no success. I was beginning to feel like a failure. Unlike other women who conceived with such ease, my body didn't seem to be working. There were many times I gave Jason the option to leave. I knew he wanted children and I wasn't able to give any to him. I was prescribed an anti-depressant due to all the stress, anxiety, and overwhelming feelings. I didn't want to take any medication, especially if I got pregnant, but the ups and downs of fertility treatments were taking a toll on my body and my marriage.

The fertility drugs brought on horrible side effects; hot flashes, cold sweats, mood swings, visual disturbances, and nausea. I thought I was going crazy. These side effects compounded the issues we were having with my body and in our marriage. When I started to see "floaters" in my eyes, the doctor immediately stopped the medication and sent me to a reproductive endocrinologist. Apparently, the dose of the medication I was on (Clomid) was higher than the manufacturer recommended. It was doing more harm than good.

I spent several more months on treatments. My reproductive endocrinologist put me on Clomid coupled with an insulin sensitizer. I started taking Metformin; however, I ended up in the hospital due to severe diarrhea and vomiting. After spending a night of recovery in the hospital, my medications were changed to Clomid and Actos.

On this combination, I began to ovulate but still wasn't pregnant. I was beginning to get depressed. We had been trying for over three years and not once did we conceive a baby. In addition to the stress of not getting pregnant, our insurance was about to change. We would no longer have infertility coverage. That meant we had one last chance to get pregnant. On the fifth attempt, with intrauterine insemination, we conceived. Our son, Joey, was born nine months later after only four and a half hours of labor. He was truly our miracle baby. The labor was so fast that I didn't feel I had time to process what had happened. I remember the first time I looked at him. As I wrote Joey's birth story this excerpt was included a week following his birth.

I held you for the first time. You were truly amazing and beautiful. You were perfect. Your color was pink and you weren't scrunchy in the face like most newborns. Your father touched you and we were all in shock at what just happened. We were in awe of you. How could two people make something so perfect? We love you so much already!

Jason and I were so happy. We finally had the child we had been dreaming of!

Up until Joey's birth I had been working administrative jobs. Once my husband started his police career I, too, wanted to become a police officer. Coming back to the civilian life after a rigid military life was difficult. I missed the structure and camaraderie of the military. A police career seemed like middle ground because it incorporated the best of both worlds. Unfortunately, I lacked the 60 hours of college credit many police departments required. I began going to school while I was pregnant. I wanted to be ready so that I could apply anywhere.

Following Joey's birth I stayed home for five years and ran my own business as a professional birth assistant (doula) and childbirth educator. This was a stepping stone for me while attending college, and I enjoyed helping women and learning about birth. Joey's birth was my inspiration. I had never known a birth could happen the way his did — so quickly. I wanted to save women from the feelings I had, as though I had been robbed of the full birth experience.

I felt like I had been misinformed. At each childbirth class, I was told that labor was 14 hours. It seems silly to believe now, but at the time I fully expected to be in labor for a full 14 hours. After a four and a half hour birth, with contractions that were constant instead of like waves, I wanted to inform as many women as possible that birth comes in many varieties.

Once Joey was ready for kindergarten it was time to pursue my police career. It seemed like the perfect moment, and I had the perfect family. I had been married to my husband for 10 years and Joey was five. Although we had always wanted another child and Joey had been praying for a baby sister since he was three, this was something we couldn't make happen for him. I had attempted fertility treatments two years after Joey was born, but we were never blessed with another child. Years of infertility treatments had taken their toll on me. I had to move on.

After five years at home, however, I wasn't sure I had the "guts" to face a job that came with confrontation. I had served four years in the Marine Corps, but that was 10 years ago. The only sure way of knowing I still had the guts was to find a job that required confrontation. I wanted one that wouldn't put me in too much danger. I began to search for a job in security.

My mother-in-law shared the name of the security company that worked in her hospital. I applied and hoped to be placed in her hospital because it was large and I would see her from time to time.

God had other plans for me.

I submitted my application on a Wednesday evening, and the next morning received a phone call asking me to come in immediately for an interview. I was offered the job on the spot. I wasn't assigned to my mother-in-law's hospital, which in hindsight was a blessing. Instead, I was assigned to my local hospital and it was only 10 minutes from my home. This spared me a 45 minute commute. My shift also allowed me to share days off with my husband. Things couldn't have happened more easily for me. I felt good. I felt wanted.

I was also very scared, especially of that next step — a real job that required me to show up on time each and every day. This was much different than working my own hours and taking on clients when I wanted. Now I would be chained to a set schedule. My doula business offered me flexibility while earning a light income, so tackling a regular job brought its own set of worries.

I took the leap of faith and started the job, immediately feeling like I belonged. It was exactly what I needed. I preferred being back in uniform. Over the next year I was taught many different tasks and had opportunities for growth. The challenges varied, from fights with drunk or suicidal people to helping the sick and injured. I was able to incorporate my compassion for others with my need to enforce rules and regulations. I really enjoyed it.

I began to apply for police positions. Unfortunately, my employment opportunities were limited. I didn't have a police certification and had to apply at departments that offered the certification. Those departments had significant physical fitness requirements that I never seemed to master. It's as though once I left the Marine Corps I could no longer run fast enough. Or that

I didn't have the motivation or drive to force myself to compete that way. It looked as if I would have to pursue another avenue: a college academy.

After a few months of research and talking extensively with my husband about which academy would best serve my needs, I chose a college police academy with instructors who taught at my husband's police academy. I submitted my application and within a few months was accepted. Four days after I started the academy, I was also accepted to a sheriff's department academy. It was a very difficult decision. I hated to turn down an opportunity with the sheriff's office. They simply didn't offer the state certification I sought, meaning it could be years before I could truly achieve my goals. That was the motivating factor to continue with the college police academy. I wasn't sure I made the right decision, but I had to go with my gut. The academy went as well as expected. I was the only cadet to graduate Summa Cum Laude!

I had an excellent prospective police department that I was in the hiring process with nearly from the start of the academy. It looked like I was going to be hired. Many officers put in good words and talked to the Chief about me. They wanted me to work there. Unfortunately, it was a shock to hear I was cut from their list shortly after graduation. There was no explanation as to why they didn't take me. I received a form letter saying they'd moved on with other candidates.

The blow was huge.

In my disappointment I just couldn't understand why I wasn't hired. Before the New Year started I put in more applications. I was accepted into the hiring process with all the departments. Within the next five weeks I would test and interview with four departments. Jobs were few, far between, and extremely competitive.

I began the testing process with a small police department just south of my town. The morning began with a written exam. By the afternoon, my life changed dramatically. I passed the written examination and knew I would be asked back for more testing. The afternoon was slotted for their physical agility test. While I didn't consider myself a couch potato, I wasn't a star athlete either. I placed myself near the end of the line and watched 180 people run the test, all passing with time to spare, including women. I felt the test would be no issue for me. I had "stage fright" but reminded myself of the time I tested for a large metropolitan police department in 2000, running faster than most of the men. Observing all these prospective recruits pass gave me confidence.

The course took place in a parking garage in the middle of a small town. We were on the second floor of the garage and, despite being the middle of the day, it was dark, chilly, and everything echoed. The course started at a police car and involved climbing over four hurdles, running around a corner, crawling under a desk, running around another corner, climbing up a six foot fence, jumping off the other side, running up and down a flight of stairs, moving a 180 lb. dummy about 20 feet, running to a bag and hitting it with the baton 20 times, and then turning around and running back to the car.

I had exactly three minutes.

As my turn approached my nerves kicked in. I knew that my anxiety would let up once I got in the car — pretty typical for me. For instance, there had been times when I literally caused myself to have diarrhea. My stomach would become a butterfly aquarium as I faced a roller coaster or performed in front of a large group. Yet, as soon as I sat in roller coaster or took the stage I instantly felt better.

I heard my number called and stepped into the car.

The officer in the seat next to me was nice. He looked like your average police officer — no facial hair, military haircut, police uniform. He shared his name, shook my hand, and gave a gentle smile as he reviewed the course and asked if I had any questions. He told me to start when I was ready. I took a deep breath and off I went! I opened the car door as fast as I could and ran towards the first hurdle. Hurdle number one complete! I approached hurdle number two in the same fashion, over, twist, run . . . but instead I felt a pop, heard a snap, and collapsed.

Two officers on scene yelled at me to get up and move. I felt like I was in Marine boot camp all over again. The officers might as well have been drill instructors, standing over me and yelling at me as if I was a piece of dirt. Another officer approached me and said to get off the course because they needed to finish. I couldn't move. I was in too much pain. I rolled around on the ground, cursing. At that point the officer realized I was severely injured. He lifted me up and assisted me to a car, calling rescue.

Rescue came, but I insisted on trying the course again. The paramedics were hesitant, recognizing my signs of injury. But I had them bandage my leg and approached the officers to beg for a retry. Unfortunately, the paramedics had no Ace wraps and instead used Coban, a stretchy elastic wrap that adheres to itself, often used like tape. Binding my knee with it wasn't appropriate. I could feel it cutting off the circulation in my leg. Not good.

After I requested a re-attempt several times, the officers called the Lieutenant and allowed it. I asked the paramedics to stay, just in case I hurt myself again. As I sat in the car the officer next to me offered some encouragement. He asked me if I was sure I wanted to do this. I was! I forced out all the negative feelings and pushed away the pain. I was determined. This might be my only chance and I needed to do this.

I opened the car door and ran towards the hurdle. I grabbed the hurdle with both hands and wanted to fly — only to collapse again. The officers didn't even look at me. They immediately began cleaning up. The paramedics came to my side. I just started crying. I was done, possibly forever.

I felt like all my options were exhausted. I had tested for six different police departments since 2000. I had gotten very close to being hired, only to learn I was cut. Now, I was cut before I even got a chance to show what I was made of. I had failed, once again, to achieve my dream. This test was so simple, and I hurt myself badly enough to ruin future opportunities to test physically. I was broken. My leg just hung there, flapping in the wind. It was dead.

I refused transport and had my friend drive me to the hospital where I worked. I was sure I would receive good treatment but felt embarrassed that people I knew had to see me like this. Would they think I was a failure? This is how I perceived myself, so I automatically assumed they would agree. In retrospect, they were as concerned and devastated for me as I was.

After an hour or so I was released without an MRI. I was referred to my HMO for an MRI and learned several weeks later that I had completely torn my ACL.

I needed surgery. Somehow, I knew I would never be the same.

Chapter 2

I had no idea what was in store for me, and just six weeks later my world erupted into chaos. My surgery was scheduled for the end of March. My husband and I had a wonderful twelfth anniversary planned at a Las Vegas resort. We would be back from the trip within a few weeks of the surgery. Afterward, I would be set to apply at police departments again.

When we returned from Las Vegas, I could tell there was something going on within my body. I felt a presence inside me that hadn't been there before. My breasts were sore, but they would get this way before my period. It couldn't be the sore breasts that whispered something was brewing in my womb. I had a sense, but wouldn't listen to it. I had never "fallen" pregnant. I kept thinking back to a few weeks prior. My husband

and I had made love . . . and I began to wonder. Could it be?

Wednesday, March 18, 2010

I told a friend of mine from the police academy that I was pregnant. I sent her a text message telling her my police career was over. She knew I was being dramatic and sent supportive messages. Then I sent a message to my sister. I was then off to buy another test because I didn't trust the first. I ended up with a digital test and had to take it in the office of the acupuncturist I was seeing that afternoon. Acupuncture was supposed to help reduce the swelling in my knee for the surgery. In the restroom I peed on the stick and waited patiently while the hourglass "thought" and then displayed PREGNANT.

I went to the acupuncturist's office and filled out the paperwork. I had never seen this acupuncturist before and I wasn't sure I could share all my thoughts and feelings with a stranger but it seemed inevitable.

She called me into the room and I just started crying. We talked a bit and she helped calm me down by putting needles in certain points of my body. It made me feel much better. Then I was off to tell your daddy the news. I didn't have much time before I had to go to work, yet I wanted to make it special for him. The best I could do was to place your positive pregnancy test in a gun case and taking it to the range. When I arrived, I was in my security uniform and there were a bunch of police officers there. The regular range staff was there. "Mario" was giving me crap for being a security officer and being in the office. John, the gunsmith, was happy to see me and was nice. Fazio was also there and was very welcoming. I held the case in my hands. I told them I needed to speak to your daddy. He was nowhere to be found. No one seemed to know where he was. They were anxious to find out what was in the gun case.

John pulled me into his office and tried to grab the case. I kept telling him he didn't need to know what was in there and that he would find out soon enough. Fazio just wanted to know what it was and kept pressuring me to tell him. "Liz, just tell me what's in the case," he would say. I asked him to find your daddy. He went looking but couldn't find him. I then asked him to check the restroom and that's where daddy was. I patiently waited for him to meet me in the office.

As I waited, I felt very nauseous. I knew your daddy would be happy and very excited . . . but I wasn't at the moment and I felt like I would disappoint him and ruin his happiness. Your daddy came out of the bathroom and was very surprised. I asked for some privacy and they let us go into the armory. Once inside, I handed your daddy the case and told him that what was inside would change his life forever and would be the most amazing thing he had ever seen. When your daddy opened the case, excitement overcame him. He began to cry and said, "Are you shittin' me?" I said, "No!" and started bawling. He knew that I was upset because your presence was another bump in the road toward my journey as a police officer.

He was very excited though and had tears of joy. He told everyone in the office and they began giving us hugs and congratulating us. Later that night, Jason told his entire family. I told my parents while I was at work. We both agreed not to tell your brother until we were together.

Over the next few days I was going through a lot mentally. I was beginning to let go of my dream and open my heart to a new one. Learning how excited your daddy was helped. He had already picked out names for you and was now treating me like a queen — something that had been lacking in our relationship for a long time.

When I discovered I was pregnant it seemed like another mountain to climb. My entire adult life seemed to be one giant mess, one obstacle after another. How many mountains would God put in front of me before He blessed me with my dream? I began to think that being a police officer wasn't God's plan for me. What if I was chasing the wrong dream? This revelation is what helped turn around the negative thoughts surrounding my pregnancy. I began to surrender to a new plan, but it came in slow stages.

While our families were excited and happy for me, I felt depressed and angry. They couldn't understand why I felt this way. Despite feeling angry, I still wanted to make it special for Jason. I liked that I surprised him at work because he was completely and joyously taken off guard. The hugs and congratulations from John and Fazio were the icing on the cake, especially because they instructed me at the police academy. They, above all, knew what I had been through and what I was trying to achieve. The news didn't seem to faze them at all. I seemed to be the only person who was taking the pregnancy so negatively. Why? Why couldn't I see it the way everyone else did?

It was extremely difficult to get through the earliest weeks of my pregnancy. I was so lost and confused. I knew that my bad thoughts and regret were not good for this new soul growing inside me. My baby needed me. Would I kill this baby with my regret?

I had huge amounts of guilt. I should have been extremely happy. It took so long for us to get pregnant with Joey and I should have been grateful for a pregnancy that didn't require fertility drugs. Even after Joey was born, we tried for four years to conceive another child. I tried every fertility method on the market from Western medicine to Eastern medicine. Nothing worked. This pregnancy happened naturally, the way it was intended. Yet, I was so distraught over the timing that I lost track of what really mattered most.

I knew I needed to make a change. I began to accept that God had intentions for me that I couldn't understand. I felt I needed to open myself up to what was in store and began to rearrange my life. I'm one of those people who always needs a plan. I don't "do" spontaneous well. While I like surprises, a surprise of this magnitude wasn't anything I had ever imagined. I focused on relishing in the joy my husband felt about this new life. Eventually I found myself becoming excited and happy about the future.

Chapter 3

I learned you were growing inside me on a Wednesday. The next day I had some blood tests taken and it was confirmed that you were present in me. That Friday I tried to make plans to get a desk job and that night we told your brother about you. He was very excited about you. All that night he couldn't stop talking about you. He had all these ideas and things in his head that he would like to do with you. He was happy he wouldn't be alone anymore.

The next day, I decided that I would announce your presence on Facebook. Moments after I posted about you and was talking to all kinds of people about you that were excited and calling you a miracle, I began to bleed. I immediately deleted the post and prayed. I felt I was losing you.

Over the next week, I spotted off and on. I had two more tests to see if you were growing . . . and you were. Last Thursday, I had an ultrasound and we saw your sac. The Doctor said things were progressing normally.

The next day, your Uncle got married. We got to see the family and everyone was excited and talking about you. I, too, was excited. I have been thinking more and more about you and I have made plans for you.

I have held myself back from taking full enjoyment of your presence. I have held back from buying things for you. I have held back because I am afraid of losing you. Today I started bleeding bright red again. There are no cramps, but I am so scared that I am losing you. Everyone has offered things for us to help you and support you and I feel that I am going to lose you.

Every day that I see blood, I am completely stressed and freaked out. I cannot think of anything BUT you. I love you and I don't even know you. I want you to grow inside me. I want to feel you grow inside me. I don't want to lose you. I don't want to lose you for many reasons, but the main reason being that you are a miracle and I believe that God has blessed us with your presence. I hope that this blessing is permanent and not something that will be taken from us.

My relationship with your father has been hard over the last few years. I have prayed and prayed that things will get better between us and your presence has created what was missing in our lives. I cannot go back to the way things were. I will die.

My sweet baby, please don't leave us. Please continue to grow. I cannot bear to lose you. Every day I wonder; will it be today that I lose your blessing? Every day is another day where you have a chance to grow. Please continue to grow strong and healthy. We all need you. You're our miracle.

As if I wasn't worried enough already, Jason wanted to tell Joey that I was pregnant. Telling Joey wasn't something I wanted to do. My concern was how upset he would be if we lost the baby. I talked with Jason about it, but he really felt strongly that we needed to tell Joey. "No matter what happens, we'll handle this as a family," he said. This was a good sales pitch and I ultimately fell for it. Still, I was concerned.

Jason and I worked hard to ensure Joey was treated as an integral part of our family. When possible, Joey assisted with decision making. Of course, Jason and I didn't ask Joey what he thought about refinancing the house, but we would ask him what he thought about purchases that might affect him or other issues such as where we went on family vacations. Jason and I also worked together as a team when it came to Joey. If I told Joey "no," Jason stood by my decision, and vice versa. I understood completely why Jason wanted to tell Joey; I just didn't feel comfortable with this choice. With the concerns I had, I needed a plan in case things went the way I feared they would. It wasn't long before I bought a book for children on miscarriage — just in case I needed it.

We decided to make the night special. We ate at Joey's favorite restaurant, a sashimi place. I never thought my son would eat raw fish, but this was his favorite dish. It was a Friday night but we knew the sushi bar wouldn't be too busy. The only people in the restaurant were on the hibachi side. The lights were dim and the room was filled with a fresh scent of fried rice. Smelling the hibachi made me very hungry. I don't eat raw fish so I ordered tempura when the waitress came by. Jason and Joey ordered a large plate of sashimi.

I brought our video camera. I have preserved most of Joey's life on camera, both video and photo, and I didn't want to miss this opportunity. I wanted to capture the moment and share it with his sibling when she was older. I was saving for posterity the joyous moment when Joey learned his dream was coming true. I couldn't wait.

I have since lost the video.

While we were waiting for the sashimi I pulled out the camera, ready to record his reaction. We told him he was going to be a big brother . . . and he was in shock! He had been praying every night for years for a sibling. Some nights we would tell him that it would probably never happen. I could see the wheels turning in his little head, and then he looked down at my belly and patted it. He got a huge smile on his face and just kind of sat there. I was so in love with this moment!

I had visions of a large belly and Joey talking to his brother or sister. I further imagined Joey at the birth. I have always said we would have a home birth if I was to get pregnant again, and I could envision Joey holding his sister after she was born. Kids always seem so giddy when they get to hold a baby, Joey would be no different. Joey witnessed his cousin being born and it didn't seem to bother him one bit; I knew he would be in awe during our home birth.

I began to imagine all the fun we would have and how great a sibling Joey would be. Joey asked if it was okay to tell his friends he was going to be a big brother. I was amazed at his insightfulness and I didn't want to take this away from him so I agreed it was okay. As the days pressed on, Joey made it known to everyone that he was going to be a big brother. He reminded me daily of his new status, instructing me to eat or drink for the baby. He wanted to buy the baby clothes. He wanted to pick something up for the baby every time we went shopping. Joey had planned on the baby sleeping in his room, and told us that he would take care of the baby in the middle of the night so we could sleep. After seeing his excitement, I reverted back to my initial reservations: Did we make a big mistake telling him? I wasn't sure this pregnancy would last, and I didn't want to see the devastation on his face.

The blood tests revealed that I had low progesterone (11.6). It was even lower than when I was pregnant with Joey (15.9). My HCG numbers were good, but I was extremely worried about the low progesterone. I knew we would need to monitor the progesterone, so I asked for extra lab tests. They agreed to the lab tests, but when the numbers came back from my Friday visit they were even lower (7.4). I asked for progesterone supplementation.

This is something the doctor wouldn't accommodate. He said that there was no scientific evidence to support the use. I explained that I had supplementation for my first pregnancy, but he was adamant against it. I rushed out and bought progesterone cream from my local natural food store. I needed something, and even though I was skeptical of its effectiveness I was willing to try anything. I began rubbing the cream on twice a day as directed. The directions told me to switch the places where I applied it from time to time, but I always rubbed it on my belly.

Rubbing my belly brought me close to my baby. I enjoyed that. In the morning, I rubbed it on quickly while getting ready for work. At night it became a special ritual. I would lie on my bed, taking slow, deep breaths, imagining my baby growing inside me. I would snap the top off the pre-measured tubes and squeeze the cool cream onto my belly. I would hear the little bubbles in the cream pop as I pushed it out onto my belly, scarred with stretch marks. The cream was thick, like toothpaste, and had a sweet smell. It would take several minutes for me to rub it in. I wanted to work in every last bit so that it would be absorbed and nourish my baby. I felt administering it this way would be more effective at increasing my progesterone. It also pro-vided me with some bonding time. It seemed this special ritual was the only time I wasn't stressed or anxious. I enjoyed my nightly bonding with my baby.

After several days had passed I began to email and call doctors I hadn't seen in years in an attempt to get progesterone supplementation. Eventually, I reached a doctor who cooperated. She offered me two types; an oral form or a suppository. *Yuck!* But I asked myself which one would work better? There was no evidence to support either, so I chose the suppository because it was deposited closer to the uterus. I trusted the oral supplementation because I took that when I was pregnant with Joey, but I chose the suppository this pregnancy because I wanted the best chance at nourishing the baby.

The doctor told me to put the suppositories up my rectum, but the compounding pharmacy said they were vaginal suppositories. I was completely relieved I didn't have to take these rectally. I read on the Internet that suppositories were messy. I had to take more time out to allow them to sit in my vagina, ensuring my body absorbed it.

I was so happy to receive the supplementation, even though the doctors seemed upset with me. I felt like I was making a last ditch effort to help my baby survive.

Initially, a huge snow storm stood between me and the possibility of "saving" my baby's life. My supplementation was delayed nearly a week! I had a considerable amount of stress while waiting, worried my baby was doomed. The third round of blood work showed increased HCG (it was doubling at the normal rate) and stable progesterone (7.4). I was hoping for an increase in progesterone, but stable was certainly better than a decrease.

After receiving the results I went to my online infertility support forums and posted there. I hadn't talked on those boards for several years, but I needed information. I knew this was the best place to find others in my situation and sought out successful pregnancies with low progesterone. There were a bunch of scary stories, but there were also a few positive ones. Some women had levels around five and some even lower. The ideal level is above sixteen. I couldn't hold on to the scary stories and focused on the positive ones. The fact that my blood levels showed good growth was positive.

Jason and I continued to talk about baby names. We could only come up with girl names and I had a sense that this baby was a girl. Focusing on baby names gave me some optimism but I still secretly felt like my baby was dying and there wasn't a thing I could do to save her.

A stable progesterone level didn't provide an assurance the baby was continuing to grow. I was so frightened and didn't have anyone to really talk about my predicament — someone who actually understood what I was going through. I wasn't sure how to express my fears. A low progesterone level didn't mean instant death and my doctors didn't seem worried. But somehow I knew I couldn't trust my doctors. I knew something wasn't right.

I needed to trust myself.

I was desperate for any glimmer of hope, but I wasn't finding it on the forums or anywhere on the Internet. Jason didn't know I was feeling so anxious. I didn't want to tell him because I knew how happy he was. I wanted him to remain blissful. What would he think of me if I lost the baby? In addition, I struggled with our decision to tell Joey.

I wasn't concerned about telling family and friends if we lost the baby, but telling Joey I lost the baby was something I couldn't bear. I cried every time I thought about it. I wondered how he might think, feel, and react. I figured friends and family would help support me through the loss, and Jason could be the buffer if I was doing badly. But Joey was another matter. It was extremely difficult suffering through two different dreams, one a glorious life with a new baby and the other a life of torment surrounding a death.

Some of my birth clients from my days as a doula

had kept their pregnancies secret until the second trimester. They did this just in case they lost their babies. Although initially upset, I chose to share the news. I wanted to let the world know! This pregnancy felt like an accomplishment. It was as though I finally mastered fertility, just like other women. Becoming spontaneously pregnant was an experience I wasn't familiar with and had longed for years to emulate.

Unlike most women who don't have to "try" to get pregnant, I endured years of unsuccessful fertility treatments. Now, miraculously, I knew the exact day of conception. After five years studying pregnancy and birth, I was fully aware of the signs leading to ovulation even though I had never personally experienced them regularly.

I had begun to experience ovulation signs every 60 days or so. Jason and I had just celebrated our 12th anniversary in Las Vegas. It was a wonderful trip that we'll both remember forever. Before our trip however; I had a few days of ovulation symptoms. We had never prevented pregnancy before and were always open to another child. Yet this time as we were about to make love I verbalized that I could be ovulating. The words my husband expressed will be engrained in my head forever, and I'm certain that many women have heard this before, "You haven't gotten pregnant any other time; you won't get pregnant now," and off we went. 14 days later I had sore breasts and the stick I peed on had a plus sign.

Chapter 4

Sunday, March 27, 2010

*The bleeding is bad today. It's like a light
period and has increased since yesterday. I am
very scared! I don't want to lose my baby on
Palm Sunday. I was going to go to the Doctor
after Mass, but the bleeding stopped. That was
refreshing, but it picked up again tonight. By
11pm I found something when I wiped. I really
hope I didn't just miscarry. I have had no
cramps! What's the deal? I will call the doctor
early in the morning and get an appointment.*

*I am so scared. I am so scared that I said
something mean to your daddy. I told him,*

"Well, now we can go back to our crappy marriage!" Urgh! I didn't mean to say that but he has been so super since I have been pregnant with you. He says I have a "free 9 month pass." That's nice, but then what? ☺

He loves me pregnant and we do so well together when I'm pregnant. I guess we'll need to learn how to do these same things for each other when we aren't pregnant. ☺

I love you baby. Please stay.

Monday, March 28, 2010

After all the bleeding over the weekend, I was scheduled for an ultrasound. I was really scared. I had no idea if I had passed you last night or if you were still inside me. My gut feeling was that you were still there, but all the fears of losing you were overpowering.

At the doctor's office I tried very hard not to cry. It was difficult, though, because there were pregnant ladies all over the place and I just kept thinking you were gone. I talked to the doctor about all the bleeding. He was super nice and VERY caring. This was my first appointment with him so I was happy about that. I have a hard time bonding with doctors, so this was very welcome — especially during such a stressful time for me.

We had an ultrasound to compare the results, so that helped. The doctor tried to reassure me, but also let me know that it's still early. It's only been four days since we last looked, so there might not be much change.

The doctor put the transducer in and my uterus was on the screen! At first, I started to panic. I didn't see the sac in there. I just took some deep breaths. Within 20 seconds, there you were! Whew! That was a relief! As the doctor began to focus on your sac and enlarge the view, I began to see something in the sac. I said, "Oh my gosh! There is something in there!" He said, "Yup!" He was smiling.

I just laid there patiently waiting as he did his measurements. He then said, "This is the yolk sac." I was amazed! You GREW!! YAY! I couldn't believe there was growth with all the bleeding I had been having. Then he said, "This looks to be the fetal pole, but it's hard to tell." As we looked for things, I could have sworn I saw a little heart beating in there. It could have just been the movement of the transducer but I *really felt like it was a heartbeat. The doctor then said, "It looks like there could be a heartbeat, but I can't say so with any certainty. It's early."*

The doctor removed the transducer and I sat up. He said things looked REALLY good. He said there was good growth and estimated you to be about five and a half weeks. He said he wanted to repeat the ultrasound with at LEAST five days in between so we can see some good growth. I felt really good about things and then we started to discuss reasons for the bleeding. The doctor had none. He manipulated my cervix and tried to make it bleed during the exam and he couldn't, so there wasn't an infection. He didn't know if the bleeding was uterine or from the cervix, either.

He said that bleeding CAN be normal even though it's scary. He also said that I am at higher risk for miscarriage because of it as well as pre-term labor, but it's only a 10-15% risk of miscarriage. He said to come back if the bleeding changes, such as it's much heavier or if it's associated with cramping.

I left the office very happy! I scheduled my ultrasound which is nine days away! Urgh! I am

very happy though, and can't wait to see you
next time. I will be seven weeks then and I know
I will see your heartbeat and feel so much
better!

It was exciting to see my baby. All the fears I had of losing her seemed to melt away. Still, there was a quiet nudge, a foreshadowing, that seemed to warn that this wouldn't turn out well. I wanted that voice to be quiet. Sometimes I thought it stopped. Just when I had breathed a sigh of relief, there it would intrude . . . again. It just didn't make sense. The baby was growing normally and on schedule. Was I just overly worried because I knew more about pregnancy? Was this how all second time moms feel? I'm so anxious with this pregnancy — a very different sensation than I experienced with my first.

I remembered worrying a bit when pregnant with Joey. But this pregnancy was causing more than worry. This time the anxiety consumed me. I couldn't focus on anything and was constantly examining the toilet paper with every visit to the restroom. Would I see bright red blood this time or the yellow color of urine? Would the blood be thick or thin? Would it be brown or pink? I over-analyzed every nuance on the toilet paper, often researching the color of blood relating to miscarriage on the Internet.

I needed something to cling to. I needed to feel some sense of control. If the blood was brown, it was old. If it was red, it was new. I remember discussing this with one of my doctors, who made it sound as if it was normal for second time moms to be this worried. If that's the case, I thought, I don't want more children. This worry was taking over my life.

After this appointment I started signing up for baby magazines and samples online. I knew my baby was growing, and I wanted to start preparing. I continued to remind myself that I thought I saw a heartbeat. I knew that once there is a heartbeat, the chance of miscarriage significantly reduces. I also started telling more people that I was pregnant, and I began interacting more on the Internet forums.

At this point one of the girls in my online group, who had been trying for years to get pregnant, had already lost her baby. I was still pregnant. I felt bad for my own relief — relief that my baby was still alive while hers wasn't. I found myself clinging to anything that would help me avoid the red reminders in my underwear . . . reminders that maybe everything might not turn out alright. Deep down I felt a bit guilty being excited about my pregnancy after I read about her loss, a terrible reminder of how fragile new life is. I made an effort to support her, but I still didn't understand how it felt to lose a baby. I hoped and prayed I would never have to understand.

I prayed so much during this pregnancy. I prayed morning and night, pleading with God that everything would turn out okay. I'm Catholic and my faith is a big part of who I am. Yet I had never prayed like this before. I had never talked to God like this before. When I was pregnant with Joey, every night I would say the same prayer, "God, please bless this baby. Help this baby to grow strong, healthy, and to full-term." I would say nearly the same thing with this pregnancy, but somehow, I just didn't believe it. There was always a thought in the back of my mind, taunting me that my efforts would be fruitless.

Despite having these doubts I still wanted to bond with my baby. There were nights I would just rub my belly and imagine her growing. My husband and son would rub my belly and talk with the baby. Joey was mostly concerned about me and asked if I was eating and drinking for the baby. There was always something "extra" I needed to do for the baby in his young mind. If I ate, I also needed to eat for the baby. It warmed my heart to already experience him being such a good big brother. I hoped this would be the beginning of his growing relationship with his little sister.

Chapter 5

Thursday, April 1, 2010

Yesterday was a blood-free day. I was finally excited, and I was "nesting." I went to the furniture store to buy some things that we've needed for quite some time to help situate the house. I brought a friend with me and it was a good day. I got what we needed, but I'm still missing another shelf for all the DVD's. At least that was the inexpensive part of the whole trip. It's time to put some stuff up for sale so we have funds to replace things.

I haven't been to work in 4 days because of the bleeding. Yesterday I decided to take a day for myself and it was a GREAT time. The weather was nice and I was able to enjoy shopping, friends, and dinner with my family.

I put in for a transfer from one hospital to another. The other hospital will offer me a day shift with weekends off. I really hope I get that. I am interviewing with the program manager today. I worked for him once when I floated there and he asked me to join his team, but I had already been assigned to another hospital.

When I woke up this morning, there was more bleeding! WTF?!?! I'm really getting upset about this bleeding. It needs to stop permanently! I am really starting to get excited about you and I want you to continue to grow.

I have another ultrasound next week. We'll see how much you have grown then. I can't wait. Until then, I'll try hard not to buy anything for you. Friends and family keep bringing us baby things and I'm only six+ weeks! It's nice to know that people care, but I feel like I have to perform and work hard to keep you inside me. I hope all works out and by Thanksgiving we are all together.

Welcome to this place!

Friday, April 2, 2010

I got the job! I will get the transfer to another hospital! I hope that helps things. Seriously, right now I don't even want to go to work. I will work directly with my supervisor and be more involved in things again. The hospital is closer to home and the hours will work well for my family. The hours will be bad if I lose you and move on to interviewing at police departments again, but you are the path that I'm following now so I am going with what's best for you.

Today, I had no blood. I REALLY hope that this is the end of it. If I don't experience anymore blood then I will know that it was just like a period because the bleeding mimicked a period. It stayed for 5-6 days, stopped one day, and then bled one more day. I really hope it's over.

I am getting SUPER excited now and just want you to grow. I want to see my belly expand and feel you inside me. It was so great feeling your brother grow inside me and I enjoyed every moment of it. I can't wait to experience that with you. Please stay, baby! I continue to pray for you.

Sunday, April 4, 2010

Today is Easter Sunday. We don't have to go to church today because we went to the Easter Vigil last night. It was a three hour service. Your brother basically slept on me all night, which was great! I haven't been able to hold him like that in a long time. I realized that if you stick, I won't hold him next year, I will be holding you, instead. That's exciting AND sad at the same time. Your daddy plays at the service, so he isn't there to help. Maybe next year your grandma will come with us.

I got up this morning feeling tired for the first time in a while. I know I will take a nap later today. Your brother got his Easter basket and he found almost all the eggs in the house. He is waiting for daddy to get up to help with the last egg. As I was making breakfast, I felt some "leakage." I am a FREAK, so I had to check. It looks like I might be starting to spot again. So far, it's not bright red so I hope it just stays this way but I am a bit crampy this morning, so I am worried.

I have been crampy before. Cramps don't necessarily mean much. I had them when I was pregnant with your brother off and on. It's my uterus growing and expanding, making space for you and providing nourishment, but I don't want it to be coupled with bleeding, so I hope this is nothing and that it goes away soon.

I go back to work today. YUCK! Working on Easter! It's my last week at my old hospital and then I will start at the new one. I looked up childbirth classes and sibling classes yesterday. I really need to stop because I need to make sure you are growing well. I just want to start doing things and preparing. I like to be prepared. I just don't want to lose you and have all this stuff to deal with either. I will continue to pray for you baby. Please don't leave us.

Please don't leave us! This was a sentence I said many times each day throughout my pregnancy. I have always considered myself to be quite intuitive. Sometimes it's been very useful, like when I have been on a police call and I felt like a suspect was lying to me or thinking about hurting me. In those situations there was body language I was "reading." But I also imagine it to be that voice inside a person's head that warns, "Don't hire this person," or, "Drive a different way to work today." There is no conscious reason for it. You just

49

"know" things aren't the right or won't work out.

Is this true intuition?

Intuition is defined as unconscious knowing or sensing without using rational processes. This makes me sound like I was irrational, but that's not how I felt. It was as if a tiny voice inside me warned of getting overly excited . . . because things were going to end poorly. How is this possible?

The psychological phenomenon of intuition is also referred to as a "sixth sense." This didn't feel like a sixth sense. This felt like conscious fibers sending signals throughout my body. It was like a physical conversation with someone telling you bad news that you refused to believe. It was that real for me.

Was my baby talking to me? Was my baby trying to prepare me?

Having such a strong feeling that my baby might die and at this point having to consciously deny it was — impossible. I felt like I was living in the world of limbo or at the "edge of hell." In my Catholic faith there was a belief that the souls of babies who died before they were baptized lived in this state. I didn't believe my baby would be subjected to this, but I felt like this is where I was living. I didn't know what was right, and felt I had no mortal direction.

I always told myself to follow my intuition as much

as possible, but there have been times when I questioned it. Sometimes I thought my intuition was speaking to me, when, in reality, it was really just past "voices" from childhood or my "self-esteem" issues. It has sometimes been difficult to tell the difference between intuition and other feelings. How did I know that I wasn't just fearful of the new journey ahead of me?

I was scrambling for any bit of control. I could control where I worked and what plans I was making for this baby, but I couldn't control the bleeding. This meant I couldn't control the black hole spinning in my stomach, telling me that my baby was going to die. I would have done anything to make that feeling disappear.

Chapter 6

Monday, April 5, 2010

Well, yesterday took a turn for the worse. I got up to take a shower and I had a huge gush of bright red blood and some small tissue came out. It was a little smaller then the size of a pea but it was firm and looked like a piece of placenta. I didn't know if this was you or part of you. I should have taken pictures of it. I know that sounds gross, but through all my searches on the internet to see what people have had come out I could only find a woman who posted the picture of her baby that came out at about 12 weeks. This is different. I didn't think it was your sac, but I am scared.

I told your daddy we were going to urgent care. We rushed out of the house. It was a LONG drive. I had to pack all my stuff for work because it was getting so late that I didn't know if I would make it to work on time or not. I didn't want to go, but I couldn't call off at this point. It was too late. So I KNEW I would have to go.

I got to urgent care and was checked-in relatively quickly. They were all supportive. I couldn't keep my tears in so I just let them flow. The doctor came in almost an hour later though. That's when we discovered they didn't have an ultrasound machine, and even if they did she wasn't an OB and couldn't do it, anyway. I was devastated. She offered a vaginal exam but I wanted to know if you were still in there. I didn't need that. She said there were still things she could do to tell, but I just didn't want that. I wanted an ultrasound. Your daddy did great by advocating for me. He got a note from her so we can try to get our co-pay back since they couldn't do much for us.

I left feeling completely empty and lost, and now I had to work for 8 hours! I assumed I would be in the vehicle all night, so off I went.

And yes, I was in the vehicle all night so I was all alone and could suffer in silence. Some of my coworkers knew something was up because I wasn't cheerful when I came in and just signed in and walked out. My boss talked to me later and I let him know what was up. He said he was sorry and asked if there was anything he could do. Unless he had an ultrasound, there wasn't.

The blood seemed to stop after the episode, so maybe I just needed to pass something. I went about my evening but ended up getting diarrhea. I think it was from the Taco Bell I ate before work, but it could also be from all this stress. I usually don't eat that crap but what I wanted isn't open on Sundays and I needed something quick. I was in an area of the hospital that didn't get service, so as I came out of the restroom I saw my Sergeant was looking for me. He said my radio wasn't working and he was about to call a search party for me. That would have been scary. I went out to my car and just dealt with things.

As I got up today, I called for a morning appointment and actually got one. I hope we see you inside me with your heart beating. That will help me feel much better. Then I need to ask what this stuff is that keeps coming out. It's scary. Just when I got used to the bright red bleeding, this happens . . . again!

I hope you are okay. I am losing faith but I continue to pray.

UPDATE: I just got back from the OB's and there you were! Your heart is beating! I could see it definitively! It looked like a normal rate but the doctor didn't measure the beats. She just wanted to check and see if you were still in there. You were bigger, too! It's GREAT! I could really see more of you this time. She guessed I was about six weeks. I am about seven now, so that's about right. I am just so happy! But I am still bleeding and afraid to lose you.

The doctor thought that maybe you implanted on a blood vessel and that's why I am bleeding. She had no suggestions for the tissue though. She also said that the risk of miscarriage is much lower now. She had me set up my first OB appointment in two weeks. It feels like that's going to be FOREVER! I can't wait! I hope you grow, lil' bean!

I was so afraid you weren't going to be in there anymore and I'm so happy you are! Off to take a nap and let all this soak in!

At this point I became completely involved and excited about my new life. Even though I still had thoughts in the back of my mind that I might lose the baby, I tried to put those doubts behind me. The heartbeat meant the risk of miscarriage was extremely low. Right? I was beginning to think that the progesterone cream was working, and all was going to be well.

Looking back, I remember having a concern that the heart rate wasn't fast enough. The doctor didn't measure my baby's heart rate, so I'll never know. I wish I had found out. I wish I had instructed the doctor to check that out or at least listen to it. I only saw the baby's heart beating. There was no way to use a Doppler to listen to the heart rate, but the audio could have been turned on through the ultrasound machine.

Still, I came home completely excited about the pregnancy and couldn't wait to share everything with my family. I wished I had brought home a picture of the baby so I could show Joey. I really wanted him to experience this growth. We got on the Internet and I showed him pictures and images of babies at his sibling's stage of development.

We read about what parts of the baby were forming and found objects around the house to compare to the size of the baby. This became a nightly ritual for both of us. I still felt sad at times when my intuition whispered that my baby might die. I did all I could to smother those whispers and allow myself to love this stage of my pregnancy.

Each night I prayed and dreamt about the new life inside me and the new life ahead. I dreamt about how Joey would love his sister and how great of a big brother he would be. As things progressed, I continued to tune out negative feelings. I was adapting to the adventures ahead. It was time to focus on this baby and to send positive vibes to the growing person inside me.

The bleeding was the worst part of this pregnancy. It felt like an intruder in my womb and its mission was to destroy any thoughts of happiness. I never knew when it was going to start or when it would stop. I hated wearing a maxi pad all day, every day. Instead of nine months free of the feminine hygiene "diapers" we endure, it seemed I was destined to spend every day adhered to one so I wouldn't destroy every pair of underwear I owned. Plus, I began to worry about getting an infection because of the lack of air to such a sensitive area.

To top it off, the vaginal suppositories were seriously inflaming my vagina. It was the most uncomfortable part of the pregnancy. I would struggle to put in the suppository because my vagina was so swollen, and then I would have to immediately lie down. I had been told this wasn't necessary, but I didn't think the medication would work if I stood up and let it all run out. I wanted to do this right, and I wanted to make sure I was providing the nourishment my baby needed. I just wished the bleeding would stop.

Chapter 7

Tuesday, April 06, 2010

My dear baby, I am emotional today. I am spotting bright red blood again and I am scared. I don't know if I will ever get used to this bleeding. I hope that you continue to stick. Tomorrow I go in for acupuncture, so I hope that helps give you what you need and also stops this bleeding. I think I will pick up an herb today as well. I need to do all I can. I know I need to have faith. I DO have faith but with my online friends losing their babies, I am worried that I will lose you too. I love you . . . Mom.

Wednesday, April 07, 2010

Well, my friend picked up False Unicorn Root yesterday and I took some last night. I hope it helps. At the very least, I hope it helps calm some of my fears. I also have acupuncture today, so that will also help. She's going to do Moxa on me and that will help tremendously. I really think part of this is hormonal and hope to find out soon. If this really helps, then I will know.

Last night I was TOTALLY freaked! ALL NIGHT! All I kept thinking about was losing you. I was making plans like you were already gone — who I needed to call and how to get surgery set up and such. I don't know why I am doing this to myself. Why is this so consuming and when will I feel out of the woods? I kept researching seven week heart rates and wondering why I didn't ask for the ultrasound picture and why I didn't have the doctor measure your heart rate. Urgh! I have to stop.

So, I decided I wanted to explore why I might be bleeding mostly in the morning. Is it because of the glycerin suppository sitting on my cervix all night or is it because I am not putting on the progesterone cream six hours after the suppository? So, I got up around 6am this morning and put on the cream. I also got up a few hours after the suppository and let it run out. So far, there was no blood this morning. I have my fingers crossed. I can't imagine God blessing us with your presence just to take you away. I have your face in my mind and I am going to try to sketch it. I hope that things continue to progress and we have you safe in our arms by Thanksgiving.

Thursday, April 8, 2010

Yesterday was my last day of work at my old hospital! YAY! I also had acupuncture and instead of doing Moxa, she bled my toes. She said that the bleeding means my uterus is hot and she needed to remove the heat. The one way to do that was through bleeding my toes. It didn't hurt. It was really interesting. So this would be day two of no blood. I am VERY thankful for that. I am finally getting excited, although I am still holding myself back a little.

I don't want to get too excited and then lose you. I need to do some more praying and thinking positively. That will certainly help. I also think I should try meditating. I have never really done that before but I need to release some of this stress. Exercise would be nice too. Hmmmm . . . maybe I can start to do some of that now, since I am not bleeding.

I had several friends from my online support forum lose their babies. Each time I read about their deaths, I felt relief that my baby was still alive. Beneath the relief, however, lurked guilty feelings, as though I shouldn't be relieved while my friends suffered. I received lots of support from forum members about all of the bleeding and that helped me to feel validated. Some of the women couldn't understand how I was still functioning with the roller coaster I was riding. Hearing them talk about how strong I was made me feel cared for and understood.

At work all I could think about was my baby. I would like to say she came to me in a dream, but it was more like a day dream. I remember driving around in the patrol vehicle and thinking about her. It was a warm day and the grass around the property was green. I stopped along the side of a building where there was a nice grassy area for people to sit. I noticed a young tree in the area full of fresh spring leaves.

Rolling down the window brought the warm breeze to my face. I began to imagine myself with my daughter, playing on the grass. We were sitting on a blanket and I was holding her up, looking at her smiling face as the wind blew. Her eyes squinted. She laughed. The picture of that moment soaked into my mind and I drew her face as best I could. The picture certainly didn't do her any justice. I was just happy to envision her. That intuitive voice whispered that this would be my only chance to see her.

I had begun to hate myself for not asking the doctor to assess her heart rate, and once again, became fixated. I tried to remember how fast it seemed to beat and kept feeling like it wasn't beating fast enough. I was mentally punishing myself for not knowing the heart rate, yet I reminded myself that at least she had a heart rate, and it was clearly visible. I attempted to reassure myself. Sometimes it worked; sometimes it didn't. I began to feel desperate. If the bleeding would just stop, I wouldn't have to over-analyze everything so much and so often.

I began to reach out to anything and everything for a solution. I had to stop the bleeding. Once the bleeding seemed to stop, I would try something else in order to keep it away. False Unicorn Root: An herb used by Native North Americans to treat female reproductive issues. It was thought to help prevent miscarriage. Anything that would help, I tried. False Unicorn Root was by far the most disgusting thing I have ever swallowed. It came in an amber glass vile with a dropper. When I sucked the tincture into the dropper, it was a dark brown color with little floating specks inside. I imagined that was the root, but it looked like someone went to a stagnant pond and filled the vile with muddy water.

The tincture was also pungent. It smelled like a mixture of rotten ginger, something sweet, and vodka. It had alcohol in it so it made my spine shiver as it went down. I didn't want to cut it into juice like some people did. I just wanted to take the shot and move on. I would hold my nose, hold the dropper over my open mouth, release the tincture, and hesitate to swallow. Once I swallowed it, I ran to get fresh water. You would think I would just have a glass waiting before I took it, but I never seemed to catch on to preparing for this awful ritual. I took this several times a day, despite how gross it was. I felt like it was worth the small amount of suffering to help this wonderful miracle growing inside me.

Then there was Moxa. What the heck is Moxa? Moxa, or Moxibustion, derives from Chinese medicine. It's thought to improve blood flow to the uterus and improve the Qi. Qi is believed to be the life force that circulates around your body. Moxa has also been used by acupuncturists to turn breech babies. I had heard of Moxa for that reason alone. When I was a birth assistant, I sent clients to an acupuncturist to turn their babies. Sometimes it worked, and sometimes it didn't. But we knew it wouldn't hurt. When I researched Moxa, I was worried it didn't fit my symptoms. Needless to say, I was relieved when the acupuncturist decided to bleed my toes, instead.

I laid on the table while the acupuncturist prepared my big toes. She wiped both of them with alcohol swabs and explained that she would use a lance to open the skin and let the blood out. I was concerned that this was going to be extremely painful. After all, the points she was touching before she used the lance were right next to the nail on my big toes. I cringed right before she began, but when she lanced the first toe I didn't really feel anything except some drips of blood. The second toe was similar. No real pain, just the feeling of warm liquid dripping down my toe. She laid a gauze pad over the toes to collect the blood. I took deep soothing breaths as I imagined all the blood leaving my uterus and coming out of my toes.

Reading this now makes me feel like a crazy person. Who opts to have their toes bled these days? It's like asking for leeches to heal some strange disease or asking a doctor to assist with bloodletting. It didn't seem realistic, but at the time you could have poked me in all kinds of places or asked me to strap maggots to my body in an effort to stop the bleeding — I would have done it! I would have done anything!

Jason thought I was a nut for taking the False Unicorn Root. He watched me cringe every time and listened to my complaints. He was familiar with acupuncture, but when I mentioned that the acupuncturist "bled my toes," he was quite intrigued. It was as if I had returned to ancient practices in an effort to save my baby. Jason didn't understand the drive inside me to do everything I could to save our baby. He didn't understand the unconscious race against time I was experiencing. I secretly wished I could live in his naïve world.

Chapter 8

Saturday, April 10, 2010

Well, I have had four days with no bleeding. I am so happy that the bleeding seems to have subsided. The only issue I have now is that my boobs are not as sore this morning. More worries, right?! Seems I can't stop worrying. I believe I lost this symptom around the same time during your brother's pregnancy. I will have to double check my records.

I SWEAR I feel you fluttering in there. I know you are so small, but I know this isn't gas. It's really weird to feel, so it's either the uterus shaking or you shaking in there. I only feel it when I am bending or leaning over and placing more pressure on my uterus, so it's not like I feel it all the time. I wonder what it is? I hope it's you. I hope you are still in there growing. I won't know for another week! I can't wait for the other ultrasound. Hopefully, all is progressing normally. I love you, baby.

Monday, April 12, 2010

I had five wonderful days with no bleeding; however, last night around 2 a. m. it came back full force — bright red and scary in the middle of the night. I am beginning to wonder if it correlates with my anxiety to go to work. I start at the new hospital today and I didn't get much sleep last night. It took over an hour to fall asleep and it wasn't a good sleep. I got up around 2am and that's when I noticed the blood. The other possibility is that this is from switching the times I administer the progesterone. Since I am working day shifts, I needed to stop the midnight and noon rubs because it's just not convenient. I tried to gradually change the time over a few days, but that didn't really work well. I guess we'll see how things progress this week.

I am not happy that I am going to work so anxious and worried. At least today is orientation. That will help. I am scared that I'll have to tell my new boss about the pregnancy and request time off. He needs a reliable person. I am normally that person, but I am just so crazy on days I have blood. I need this bleeding to STOP! It's sooooo scary!

I am beginning to believe that something isn't right with you. I know it's probably just me being negative due to the bleeding, but deep down I am beginning to feel something is truly wrong. Please stay with me, baby!

Tuesday, April 13, 2010

Well, I have a strong feeling that this is it. I don't know why, but I have this feeling that you are gone. I rescheduled my first OB appointment for tomorrow, so we'll see. I have been so anxious these last few days and haven't been sleeping, so maybe it's just because I am tired or maybe just tired of wondering? I don't know. I sent a message to my friends Glenna and Tiffany stating that I think you are gone. I told Glenna that I am at peace with it. This is what was meant to happen. I told her that I had an appointment tomorrow and she hoped I was wrong. Tiffany said that she understands intuition but she hopes I am wrong, as well. Tomorrow will tell. I hope I am wrong.

I am also a bit crampy today and these are the real cramps. Something just feels "off." The bleeding may be coming back as well so I'll be watching that. I am going to try to relax tonight and hopefully, things will settle down. I have had to pee like 20 times today and that's a strong sign of pregnancy, so maybe you're still in there growing but I just don't know. I am scared and I am tired of being scared . . .

I knew this was it, but I didn't want to believe it. I needed confirmation from a doctor that my baby was gone. Looking back, I wished I had gone to the emergency department and found out that night, but there wouldn't have been much that they could've done for me. If I wasn't actively miscarrying, they would have just had me see my primary care physician the next day.

It was extremely horrifying to live in my body when I felt so deeply that something was wrong. I was desperately hoping someone would believe me and console me. But how could they? There was no confirmation to my feelings, so how could they possibly understand? I knew this was more than worry and anxiety.

I knew it was real.

My husband and I had been on this roller coaster together, but he didn't seem as involved in the anxiety as I was. I don't think my husband believed that my feelings were real. Any conversation I had with him about my worry and anxiety seemed to always be followed up with, "You're just worried because you know more this time around." It got to the point where I tried not to talk about my feelings, but I felt so alone if I held back. I really needed him to believe me. I really needed him to validate my feelings.

But if my husband felt like my feelings were real, he certainly didn't come out and say it. That was actually considerate on his part. I would have been completely crushed if he said, "Elizabeth, you're probably right! Our baby is dead!" I probably would have been angry at him for giving up, and we would have fought more over our pregnancy woes. I'll say though, after everything was over, my husband told me that he'll never doubt my intuition again.

The other feeling I experienced was peace. How could someone who wanted this baby so badly and who'd struggled through weeks of bleeding, anxiety, and worry feel . . . peace? The last few weeks were frightening. Each day I wondered whether or not this pregnancy was going to end and I felt with every fiber of my being that it would. Now I felt like I was staring into the wrong end of a gun just waiting for someone to pull the trigger so this misery would be over. Still, I felt peace. I think it was because at least I saw an end to this roller coaster ride.

Even though I clearly didn't want it to end, at least I would have a solid answer. There would be no more wondering. Even though I didn't yet have confirmation that my baby was gone, I knew it. I didn't sleep well that night, but I told my friends that I was going to be okay. I think my feelings were very similar to people who have an unknown or undiagnosed disease — they feel peace when they finally have a name for their issue. An answer. It doesn't change the fact that they could die or will live forever with symptoms, but the fact that they have a name makes everything feel less chaotic and scary.

Chapter 9

Wednesday, April 14, 2010

Well, my feelings have been confirmed. You have passed away inside me. It's really weird knowing that your body is still there but you are no longer alive. I don't know what I can give to you. I wish that I could help you.

When I arrived at the clinic, they asked me to fill out a bunch of papers. I told the receptionist that I believed you were gone and she said that she would see if I needed to complete the papers. When she came back, she said that I could complete them after the appointment. The nurse got me in quickly. Your brother was really sick. He was throwing up in the car and held his head over a bowl in the office. I asked the nurse if I should have daddy and him stay in the waiting room. She took my blood pressure and vitals and said she would put me in a room and then have them come in.

As we were getting ready to go to a room, the patient scheduled before me had just shown up . . . late. The nurse said she was just going to put me in a room and have the nurse practitioner (NP) come in so she could do the ultrasound quickly and let me know.

She put me in a room. She had me change and brought daddy and your brother in. We all sat there, waiting. The NP came in and asked me some questions. I was very emotional. I just KNEW you were gone. I explained to her my feelings and what had been happening. She did a cervical exam and stated that my cervix was VERY red. I told her that I believed the suppositories were causing that. I told her I wanted to switch to oral. She didn't believe that a doctor prescribed oral progesterone for me so we talked about that a little and then finished the exam.

She set up the ultrasound and put in the transducer. There you were . . . bigger this time than you were the last ultrasound. It was hard to believe that you had died. I could tell right away there was no heartbeat. The NP tried and tried to find one. She even turned on the audio. I said, "There's no heartbeat, is there?" I turned away from the screen. I was getting dizzy. I couldn't bear to see you anymore. I knew you were gone. After a few minutes of silence, the NP said, "No, I'm sorry. There is no heartbeat." She looked around a little more, and then we finished up.

Your brother was vomiting again, and I felt like I was going to throw up. I asked daddy and your brother to leave so I could discuss options. They left, and I was crying a lot and talking with the NP. The NP gave me all my options. She left and then brought daddy in so we could talk about the options.

I could see that daddy was very upset. That was hard. I hate to see him cry. He didn't want to make a decision right then, so I decided we would wait until tomorrow. When the NP came back in, I told her I hadn't made a decision yet. I then asked about genetic testing. She said they don't normally do it. I asked if I could have it done. She said she would ask and left. She came back and told me they could do it, and we talked

77

a little about that.

Of course, I got the . . . "This isn't your fault" and "It's a genetic problem" speech. Ugh! I didn't want to hear that. I know all about that. The NP didn't need to know why I want the testing. My goal is to ensure that it was chromosomal and not because of a lack of hormones. Part of me believes I didn't make the right hormones and that's why you died.

I may never know. I have to catch you in a container as you come out and then rush you to the lab where they'll ship you off to Texas for testing. Wow! Not even born into this world and you already get to make a flight.

I hope I can catch you. I know it will be hard. If I choose to have surgery, I wouldn't have to worry about that. I guess I'll see how I feel tomorrow.

I'm so sorry you're gone, little one. I love you and I will miss feeling you grow inside of me. Be an angel, my dear!

I just sat there; devastated, crushed. I didn't know what to think anymore. Is this what it feels like to have the sacred torn from you? I prayed so hard during this pregnancy. I prayed the rosary every day. Jason and I prayed the rosary as a family. We went to church and lit candles. I knelt often and prayed hard, yet this tiny life inside me died. I couldn't understand or begin to comprehend why. Why did God take my precious miracle from me? Even though there was some level of peace, I didn't want to believe it, and I didn't want to experience this.

The nurse practitioner must have been in an awkward position. I tried to think of things from her point of view. Why did I do this all the time, putting myself in other people's shoes? After all, this was MY moment, not hers. Maybe it was easier to put myself in her position, knowing it provided me a moment of escape from the horrifying event that was happening inside of my body. I couldn't imagine being on the other side of the table, telling a pregnant woman her baby was dead. I remember looking at her and saying, "This must be one of the worst parts of your job." She didn't say anything back, which made me feel worse.

She tried very hard to find the heartbeat. I'll give her that much. She even turned on the audio, but it wasn't there. I began to feel numb. Was this really happening to me? I just wanted to rewind and start over. The ultrasound seemed like it took forever, but I knew it was only minutes. I became extremely nauseous listening to Joey dry heave right next to me. I needed him to leave

79

quickly so I had Jason take him into the waiting area.

I just laid there, half naked atop a hard exam table with my legs up in stirrups. The room was still dark and it was freezing. There were pictures of moms with their new babies on the walls. I felt like I was in a torture chamber. So many women receive good news in this room. Where was mine? The nurse practitioner began to explain my options. I just wanted her to shut up. She could have at least told me I could sit up. The paper sheet draped over my legs was itchy, and I felt as if I was on display. It seemed as if time began to speed up. The doctor explained everything to me, but I didn't hear her. I could see her mouth moving at the speed of light; it was as if I was watching an old movie where the sound doesn't match with the video.

I knew I wanted to pass my baby naturally, but I didn't know when this would happen. I couldn't go for weeks waiting. I had already waited months for this to happen. And so I listened to my options. I just wanted to vomit as my poor son was doing. I just wanted to scream! I wanted to run away, but couldn't! I was trapped in a tiny little room with a deadly machine that just gave me the worst news ever!

After everything was explained, the only thing I knew for sure was that I wanted the baby tested. I asked about testing the baby several times. I felt they wanted me to justify why I wanted the baby tested, as if they'd done something wrong. I wanted to know two things. Was this chromosomal, and was she really a girl? I had to explain why I wanted the testing to several staff members. I felt like they shouldn't have given me so much trouble over it. I wasn't placing blame on them, and this wasn't a reflection of their care. To this day, I firmly believe my baby's death wasn't chromosomal. I believe her death was the result of a lack of pro-esterone production. Whether or not the supplemen-tation would help remains to be discovered through studies. The nurse practitioner stated she would have to get the doctor.

When the doctor came in, he said I had to have two more miscarriages before insurance would foot the bill on the test, I became so angry. I couldn't accept that! I opted to pay out-of-pocket for the tests. I was so sure that I wanted the tests and would have been willing to pay thousands at that moment.

Jason came back into the room and told me a nurse was watching Joey for us so he could cry with me. Everyone in the room left. I was still on the exam table, although I was now sitting up. I didn't really want to look at him because I hated to see him cry, and I could see tears welling up in his eyes. Jason never cried. Seeing these tears made the devastation so real. We were both in this sterile room with bright lights that seemed to shine down on us as if to say, "Look at these two people who just lost their baby!" It was as if the lights were mocking us. The table separated us enough that we couldn't hold each other. I lay back down, and Jason laid his head on my stomach, holding my hand as we cried.

It was a moment that I never want to experience again. Our baby was gone, and there was no way to bring her back. There was no CPR. There was no trying to keep this baby alive. There was no in-utero surgery. Our baby was dead. DEAD! No heartbeat. Life was gone!

Having Joey with us was really hard. I couldn't imagine what he was observing. What was he feeling? I tried to look at the day's events from his perspective. Joey was rushed from his home to the doctor's office, but instead of being seen for his vomiting, his mother was being seen. His mom was half naked on a table, we were all squeezed in a tiny room with professionals he's never met, and a strange monitor displayed the picture of our baby — HIS baby. He held a large white, mixing bowl and threw up in it periodically as his mother began to weep. Was he even aware why all this was happening? I tried not to think about any damage I may have caused Joey having him there.

My husband. My poor, poor husband, who not only had to console a sick child but also his grieving wife. All along, he had to be strong and hold in his own grief. He had received horrible news. This was something he had never experienced before. He now had to be a warrior. My husband has been a police officer for twelve years. He has seen the worst of the worst and has had to suppress his feelings and emotions during some difficult times, but being the rock for his family wasn't his forte. One of the things Jason has always loved about me was my strength. He loved that he could trust me to be the strong one at home since he had to be so strong at work.

Lately, it had been very exhausting for me to be the strong one. Jason and I had been struggling in our relationship because of this. I was concerned Jason wouldn't be able to step up to the plate and be the rock I needed him to be. I quickly learned I had nothing to fear, and I could place complete trust in him. Jason did an amazing job that day. I am extremely thankful for how he handled everything under the circumstances he was dealt. I am sure he was dying inside and certain he was mourning, though I never saw him break except for our moment together in the examination room.

It took me over forty-five minutes to get dressed, so I asked Jason to take Joey home, knowing he had driven there in his own car. Jason didn't want to leave me there. I could see the worry on his face, but I was really concerned about Joey, and I didn't want either of them with me anymore. I just needed space. I felt like I had to push him away to get him to leave. It was like the old movies where the woman has to scream, "Leave! Get out of here!" This moment was something I needed to go through on my own.

On my way out, I stopped by the lab for blood tests and to get sterile containers for catching my baby. I felt like a zombie in the lab. My face was swollen, and my eyes were red. I was on autopilot. It wasn't until after the lab tech took my blood that I realized I was going to have to ask for the containers. I didn't know how to say it. How does one ask for something to catch a dead baby in? I began crying and told the tech that I needed containers to catch my dead baby. I am sure I shocked her. She hurried off and brought me what I needed. They were clear, graduated containers that are used for urine. How disgusting! I couldn't believe this is what I had to catch my baby in! There wasn't anything larger or more suitable for catching a developing child? I left and got in my car but couldn't move. I felt so heavy.

I probably shouldn't have been driving, but I did anyway. It was a forty minute drive home. I got a call from the doctor on the way home who said I didn't have the right containers and that I needed to come back. I asked if the clinic closer to my house would have them, and she said they should, so I stopped there. They had no idea what I was looking for. I must have looked awful because a doctor there pulled me into her office for a consult. This doctor actually pissed me off. She didn't know me, and she didn't know what had just happened. Who the hell was she to pull me into her office as if I was some mental health patient?!

I began to explain why I was there and tried to hold off my tears, but I couldn't. I explained to her my internal conflict of what I needed to do to catch my baby. She didn't think I could do this, and then explained that a D&C might be better because it would be easier to collect sterile "tissue." She called my baby "tissue." I felt confused by everything she was telling me. After explaining that a D&C would ensure collecting the proper tissue, she warned me that a D&C might also ruin my uterus.

At that point, I didn't know what I wanted. I tried to explain it, but the look on her face made me feel like she thought I was crazy. I just rambled on and cried and couldn't keep my thoughts together. I thought she would never let me leave. An assistant brought in the containers they thought I needed. They were the same urine containers, but they opened them up and put in saline solution. I looked at them in confusion. How could they be sterile now? They just opened them and poured saline into them?

I called the other clinic back and asked them about these containers. They told me they weren't going to work because they had been opened, so I had to drive back to the other clinic. When I arrived, the lab director had everything I needed and gave me instructions on how to catch the baby directly into the container and then pour saline solution on top. The baby couldn't fall into the toilet, land on tissue, or on underwear as the tissue used for testing could become contaminated. I knew this would be a challenge, but I was sure I could do it.

After several hours of driving back and forth, I made it home; however, no one could prepare me for what the night would bring. I wasn't ready to let go. I knew that if I stopped taking the progesterone, the miscarriage would happen more quickly. I decided to take it again that afternoon. As the night progressed, I began to freak out. I didn't realize that I would have to sleep with a dead baby inside me until I started to relax and get ready for bed. It was surreal. I had sent text messages to all my friends and family on the way home from the clinic so I didn't need to make any calls that night. The message was simple, "My baby is dead."

Before I retired to my room for the night, I confided in Tiffany, who had had a miscarriage. I sent her a text to tell her I wasn't doing well. Little did I know she was pulling into my driveway. Her husband had brought her, which was a big deal. It made me feel special knowing he drove her out so late to see me. She made me chocolate-covered strawberries and some other comfort food. She also had a card with her. She sat on the couch next to me and just hugged me while I cried. I felt like we were reliving a moment from years back when I moved out of the neighborhood where we both had lived. I felt so vulnerable, and I don't usually let others see this kind of vulnerability in me, but somehow, knowing we had something in common, allowed me to release these feelings to her.

I told her I couldn't sleep with this dead baby in me, and we just cried together for a while. After she left, I called my sister for support. I told her I couldn't sleep with the dead baby and she told me to go to the emergency room for a D&C. I called the hospital, but they told me they wouldn't do one, so I just stayed home. I slept for two hours out of pure exhaustion, but stayed up the rest of the night researching my options.

Chapter 10

Thursday, April 15, 2010

It's 5:30am I got up a few hours ago. Last night was just horrible. Lots of crying. Jason is so upset, too. The hardest part for me is knowing that my baby is dead inside me and I am still functioning. I don't want this. It's so hard emotionally. I am not one of those people that thinks there was a mistake. I KNOW my body and I KNOW my baby is gone. There is NO mistaking this. I am awake researching my options. I really just want to get this over with. The thought of going through all the pain of passing my baby and trying to catch my baby disgusts me. I don't know what the right choice is. None of the choices seem good. Each one has negatives. I'll list them.

Waiting to naturally miscarry – This could take weeks! I just got a new job and I don't have weeks to wait. I'll feel unprepared to catch my baby. I hope I can catch my baby

Using a medication to miscarry – This could take a few days. I may not catch what needs to be caught for testing. It's VERY painful, more painful than waiting.

Surgically removing my baby – D&C. There are so many risks involved with this procedure but it's over quickly and I'll be able to test my baby.

I am not cramping right now. I am passing small blood clots; the feathery kind. I would like to wait until it's daylight to make my decision. I need to make it by at LEAST noon. That's when I'm supposed to see the doctor. I'll probably call first thing to see if I can schedule the D&C for today. It's tax day. I just realized that.

I am so sad. Words cannot describe the pain I am going through. This was a huge loss. Part of me wants to try to have a baby again, which is why I wouldn't want the D&C. But now I just want this baby out. This baby left. I need closure. Maybe I am not strong enough to deal with this? I don't know. I just need it to be over.

The word has spread through the neighborhood. An estranged neighbor sent me a text message saying she was sorry for my loss. She said that her daughter and her talked about it this morning and her daughter didn't know that something like this could happen. I miss her. I sent a few messages back and forth but I am not sure how much I can trust her so I just left it at that and didn't say that I missed her . . . even though I do.

By morning, I knew that I needed to have the D&C because it was the best option for catching my baby so she could be tested. I had called the doctor first thing that morning and told her what I wanted. She insisted I come in to see the OBGYN director and have another ultrasound. Why? Was it likely there would be a heartbeat today?

Jason and I went in anyway. Joey absolutely refused to go with us. He was feeling better, but he didn't have school that day. He refused to go to the appointment. I didn't blame him, but I had to scramble at the last minute to find someone to watch him. Joey asked for Glenna to watch him. I sent her a text message, and she was available. It was hard for me to hear Joey say he didn't want to come, but I was glad Glenna was available to care for him because there was no other person at that moment who could have helped him through this better than her. She was an angel from heaven.

When we arrived at the clinic, I was scheduled with the OBGYN director. He did the ultrasound again and confirmed my baby was dead. Was there any doubt? I didn't have any. Why did he? He took another picture of the baby and tucked it away. I felt so sick seeing this again, and I couldn't understand the purpose of this ultrasound. It wasn't explained to me either. It was pure torture. The pain was happening all over again, like pouring salt in an open wound and rubbing in broken bits of glass.

I asked about having a D&C, but the director refused to do the procedure right away and said I was scheduled for tomorrow. I told him I couldn't go through another night like last night and that the miscarriage was imminent. I felt like I would have an anxiety attack if I had to sleep with this dead baby inside me again. All I wanted was this dead baby out of me! He checked my cervix and it was closed, so he said that the miscarriage wouldn't happen tonight and I could wait until tomorrow.

I was bawling and yelling at him. I screamed, "Do

you know what it's like knowing you have a dead baby inside you?!" He told me he didn't. He had extremely good bedside manner, and I was impressed that he didn't take my statements personally and get angry with me despite all that was happening. Because of my emotions, he mostly talked with Jason, which I appreciated. When I told him I was having the baby tested, he said they wouldn't pay for it. I told him I had already paid for the test. He kept talking about how the baby's death was probably chromosomal, and I wouldn't learn much from tests. I told him I didn't care because there were other things I could be told — like the sex of my baby — and I needed the tests for me to heal.

I didn't think we were getting anywhere with him, and I didn't feel like there was any compromising, so I screamed at him, "GET OUT!" I was done processing everything, and I just needed to be left alone. I sat there on the exam table, crying, and I didn't know how to gather my thoughts. I decided I would refuse to leave the office. I was at the point where if I didn't get something, I wasn't going to leave. I wanted this baby out of me.

I asked Jason to step out. I was so furious. Jason left. I stood up and stared at the walls in the room. It felt as though everything was spinning. I wanted to rip all the pictures off the walls and throw the tongue depressor and cotton ball containers, or anything I could get my hands on around the room. I just wanted to break everything in sight. I wanted to scream. I wanted to stomp my feet and demand my baby be taken from me NOW! My baby was dead! Didn't my feelings matter? I wasn't even offered a medication to help me through the night. I felt like I was told to live with it.

After almost forty-five minutes of feeling completely numb and dead inside, I began to get dressed. I think my tears were dried up at this point. My face was red and swollen, and I didn't care. As I emerged from the room, Jason was there. He had an expression of relief on his face. Turns out, he was freaking out outside the office. He thought that I was going to go berserk and destroy the office. He was right. I was contemplating everything he was afraid of.

It seemed he knew me very well, but I was held back from pure insanity because my future with a police department was on the line. If I had destroyed anything, I could have been arrested. Even though I was nearly past caring, I couldn't destroy what was left of my future. The future, despite it being so grim that day, was still on my mind.

Thursday, April 15, 2010 at 2pm

So, I just got back from the doctor. Again, he confirmed your heart stopped beating. He said it stopped beating at six ½ weeks but I know that's wrong because I had an ultrasound after that. The NP said 7w3d. I say it was 7w6d or 8w0d. Anyhow, he was very empathetic but really ticked me off when he wouldn't authorize the chromosome testing. I KNOW this was due to my hormones and nothing was wrong with you, which makes me mad.

So, the bleeding has picked up. This morning I had this weird brown/gray thick blood. Right now, the bright red blood is flowing and there are small clots. I had a cramp that just stuck with me after the ultrasound. I didn't think much of it. Now, I can tell that I am cramping and it hurts. It's just getting worse.

It's 7:15pm now. I finally got some pain meds. The pain was getting very bad. I passed something and put it in the container and filled it with the saline solution. I don't know if it was you or not. I guess we'll find out. I am scheduled for an ultrasound first thing in the morning and then I go in for the D&C. Even though I have pain meds on board, I am still in pain. The meds aren't that strong; Tylenol with Codeine. I am allergic to opiate derivatives so they are having a hard time picking the right drugs for me. Oh well, at least I have something.

Another neighbor called me to express her sympathy. I haven't spoken to her in months. The information passed around the neighborhood quickly. It was interesting. It was nice to hear from her and nice of her to let me know she was sorry. I miss her.

The miscarriage started that afternoon. The doctor told me it wouldn't; but it did. I hated him. Labor started like any other. It started with small, short cramps and heavier bleeding. The bleeding was tarry and black. I sat in bed and tried not to move. I called the doctor and asked for pain medication. I didn't want to endure this. I sent Jay out to get the meds and took some when he got home. I wanted to take the whole bottle. I didn't want to die, but I didn't want to be alive to feel this physical and emotional pain any longer. If someone had said that they could put me out, I would have taken the offer.

I laid in bed all night. The TV was on, but I wasn't really watching it. I was just staring off into space. I

needed something to take my mind off what was happening and about to happen, but the TV didn't really do
a good job of that. I still thought about it. I still cried. I
still wept like a baby. I would just lie there, staring at
the ceiling and asking God, "Why?" *Why the hell did
this happen?*

Due to the onset of miscarriage, the doctor wanted
to see me yet again for another ultrasound in the
morning. They didn't want to do the D&C if I had
passed the baby. It felt like this was more about money
for them than true concern for me and my baby. From
this point on, anytime I got up to use the restroom, I had
to put a sterile cup between my legs and walk there
"just in case." It sucked.

Joey's labor didn't start this way. In fact, with Joey I
didn't realize I was in labor until my water broke and I
had the most horrendous pain ever. Going through a
miscarriage IS experiencing labor. I didn't realize the
similarities until the next day, but as I lay in bed, devastated and out of touch with life, I thought about the full-
term labor I would miss with this baby.

A small light was on in my room; it was like sitting
by candlelight. It was dark outside and quiet in the
house. I imagined the birthing tub placed in the bay
window corner of my room and sitting in the warm
water with my eyes closed as I swayed back and forth

with the contractions. I would moan off and on and become "one" with the earth. Maybe that doesn't sound realistic, but after attending over 100 births, I had seen this many times. I don't know if the women felt "one" with the earth, but it looked that way to me. Then, when it was time to push, I would bear down like mother earth and bring my baby into this world, actually grabbing her and pulling her from my womb, then placing her on my chest as she took her first breath. I would still be in the water, and we would just float there together. I imagined it would feel as though the world stopped turning, a brief moment suspending us in the warm water and relishing the birth of a new life.

I wasn't destined to have this experience, one I had been dreaming about for the last few years. Joey's birth was so different from what I had imagined my next birth would be like. The biggest difference was his birth was in the hospital, and I wanted my daughter's birth to be at home. The thought of home birthing, though exciting and strongly desired, also scared me because I didn't know if I was strong enough. With Joey's birth, I asked for an epidural immediately.

Joey's short birth made me wonder if this meant I might have my next baby in the car on the way to the hospital. Well, I didn't have to worry about that scenario anymore. I no longer had to worry if I was strong enough to have a natural birth. I didn't have to worry about taking classes to change my way of thinking about labor, and I didn't have to worry about choosing a midwife and doula. It was really sad, because as much as I worried about all those choices, I was at least happy to have those choices. Now those choices were gone. Now I was just ordinary. Now, my baby was dead.

Chapter 11

Saturday, April 17, 2010

Everything is over and I don't wish that on ANYONE! I actually started my miscarriage Thursday, but I stayed in bed. That kind of held it off for a little while. Then on Friday morning the doctors wanted me to come in a few hours early to check and see if I had passed the baby. THAT was a mistake. As soon as I got downstairs, I was in horrendous pain! The contractions were coming every two to three minutes and were excruciating. I kept telling Jason I would be able to do this if it were real labor . . . but this was something so sad. I just wanted to be numb.

I got to the OB, and the exam and ultra-sound were EXTREMELY painful. The baby was still in me, but the doctor said it was trying to come out. Soooo . . . I was like, PLEASE give me pain meds. THAT was the wrong thing to say and caused problems. I was also asking for my ultrasound photos. They didn't want to give them to me. Urgh! After 20 minutes of almost CONSTANT asking, they gave me the last two photos of my baby, but not without this OB say-ing, "Why, was there a fetus in there?" CRAZY BITCH! YES! I want it. So it's morbid, big deal! Give me the fucking photo!!

Then they said, "Your Doctor doesn't want to give you any pain meds." Okay, here I am on the exam table, moaning in pain, and they don't want to give me anything? Then they said, "If we give you something, we have to transport you by ambulance to the surgery center." I said, "I am NOT paying for an ambulance. They're too expensive. My hubby can drive me there." At this point, I needed to suck it up and be strong for what I wanted. After an hour of fighting with them, and me being in pain, Jason and I left. I realized that they wanted me transferred by ambulance due to my allergy to opiates. Any narcotic they gave me could cause a reaction. They needed me to be monitored. They could have said that, though, instead of being so obstinate.

I got to the surgery center. The clinic had called ahead and they got me in right away. The nurse was AMAZING and very empathetic. She got me checked in, undressed, and put my IV in quickly. Then I got some drugs. I felt much better, but the drugs only lasted 15-20 minutes each time. They kept having to administer additional doses because my surgery wasn't until 12:30. I got there at about 10:30 that morning.

I was deathly afraid I would pass my baby and not get to catch her in a sterile container, so I tried to sit as still as possible. 12:30 came and I went into the operating room. I began to freak out about it because of the kind of experience, but I just kept saying to myself, "I want to be numb, I don't want to experience this." Off to sleep I went.

Waking up was WEIRD, and they ended up intubating me because my heart rate was so low. I kept feeling my chest to see if I had died and if they had done CPR on me; but that wasn't the deal. Jason came in and told me that when the

103

doctor put in the speculum the baby was in the birth canal. They did the D&C anyway and captured what they needed for their specimen and mine. I was glad. I realized I had actually given birth to my baby before the surgery. Urgh! I wished I had had the surgery the day before and avoided all of this.

I felt instant relief. I am glad it's all over even though it's sad. The whole pregnancy has been a roller coaster, and now it's over. I don't have to stress about every twinge or drop of blood. I must have known something wasn't right from the very beginning. I didn't stress like this with Joey. So, I am just healing now, which isn't that fun, either. I am taking some time off work to heal emotionally and physically. I am flying to Oklahoma this afternoon. The love between a husband and wife that created life is now gone. The life that was proof of that love, has died. It's a very sad time.

I asked my dad to fly in from Oklahoma, and he came quickly. Knowing that he was available for me was very comforting. It seemed to heal the damage and trauma from my childhood. I wasn't close to my dad as a child, but over the last few years I had become much closer to him, and I needed his presence and advocacy. I didn't know how he would handle this situation since this wasn't an area where I shared explicit details with him, but my heart ached for him to be here and to go through this with me. He had arrived late on Thursday. Jason went to get him that night while I was home in bed.

On the morning of my D&C, the cramps and bleeding had actually stopped. I got up and took a shower before my appointment. I couldn't eat that morning because of the procedure, but it didn't matter, I hadn't eaten anything in two days, anyway. The constant knot in my stomach, coupled with severe grief, prevented me from providing my body any nourishment. After all, I no longer had a reason to eat other than for myself, and I didn't want anything.

Dad didn't want to go to the hospital with me. I had a feeling he wouldn't go, but I secretly hoped he would. I was disappointed that he wouldn't be there, but I also understood. Instead of going with us, he took care of Joey and tinkered with my car while we were at the hospital. He was being as nurturing as he could be. From a distance. I loved that he did this for us — for me.

I was feeling quite well, physically, as I prepared for the trip to the hospital for the D&C. I dreaded going to the clinic first. I felt it was unnecessary. I took a warm shower and thought about what was ahead of me that day. Since I wasn't bleeding or cramping, I had a moment where the impending doom of that day had escaped me. I decided to wear my police academy sweat pants. They served two purposes; I needed something loose to wear and it helped me feel strong.

I came downstairs and I was ready to go, but a feeling overcame me. I had had this feeling before. It was the same feeling I had when I went into labor with Joey. I knew I had only a small amount of time to leave before labor began, so I kissed Joey goodbye and told him I loved him. I began walking toward the car and real labor began. I yelled at Jason to hurry up and get in the car. I am sure this upset him. I knew he was worried about me as he processed his loss, but I was only thinking about me and what I was going through. All of a sudden I was in excruciating pain. I immediately wanted to go back upstairs, take the narcotics I was prescribed, and lay down. Yet I couldn't take anything or my surgery would be cancelled.

I was bent over, holding my belly, as I told my dad goodbye and got in the car. I had been in this position before, except the last time occurred under far happier circumstances when I was about to meet my new baby boy. This time, I had a date with death. I was scared.

Jason rushed me to the clinic. The surgery was

downtown. The clinic wasn't. I hated the fact that I had to go to the clinic only to confirm, yet again, that my baby was dead and still inside me. I wondered why they couldn't perform an ultrasound at the hospital. I thought this would be a routine procedure to do before a D&C, but it wasn't. During the car ride, I was relieved Jason didn't ask me too many questions. He just held my hand as the waves of pain possessed my body every few minutes.

I arrived at the clinic and Jason got me a wheelchair. He pushed me into the clinic as I held my belly, moaning in pain. I hated that we had to sit in the waiting room like everyone else while I was in this condition. I couldn't imagine what people were thinking of me. I looked like I was in labor, but I didn't have the belly to show it. It was embarrassing, and I just wanted to hide under a blanket. I hid my face in my sweatshirt. I didn't want to make eye contact with anyone. I felt like I would scream, "My baby's dead!" if I made eye contact with anyone.

Jason took care of checking me in, and I finally made it to a room. They set up the ultrasound machine. This was the dreaded machine. It was now the machine of death for me. I realized at this moment that the ultrasound machine can bring many different types of news to people. Confirming pregnancy. Identifying the sex of the baby. Measuring the baby. Checking for anomalies. Confirming death. How could a machine have this much power? How could this machine bring good news and bad news? I just wanted it to be over.

The ultrasound was excruciating, both physically and emotionally. I didn't want to look, but I did. There she was! The baby was still in my uterus. It was time to go downtown. I was in so much pain. They finally offered to order pain meds, and I gladly accepted. Every two minutes, like clockwork, I was in misery. I couldn't imagine what the guy on the other side of the wall in the waiting room was thinking, listening to me in such pain, but I didn't care. It hurt. I hurt.

It seemed like forever for them to come back with the medication. Instead of pills, the nurse brought me some bad news. She had called the doctor who told them not to give me anything. I was so angry! Why? I didn't understand. I was in serious pain, and I was being denied pain medication?! I also couldn't believe they had to call a doctor. Wasn't a doctor present? I became very angry and nearly belligerent with the staff. They finally explained why I couldn't have pain medication. I have allergies to certain medications, and they couldn't risk a reaction in the office.

Then the nurse told me I had to be transported via ambulance. I absolutely refused. She said she already called for the ambulance. I told her that if I was going to go to the surgery center in pain, I wasn't going to pay thousands for a ride. I felt victimized at this point. I just wanted to get out of there. Here I was, in this tiny room again, surrounded by pictures of moms and their new babies, living the last three days over again, and I wasn't being heard. Miscarriage is so common, and I was confused as to why this nurse was giving me such a hard time and wasn't empathetic to my situation.

For instance, I had asked for the ultrasound pictures the night before, but they hadn't given them to me. So I asked for them once again. She refused to give them to me. This was really getting ridiculous. I felt as if my experience didn't matter to them. They wanted to do what they wanted to do. As much as I wanted to leave, I didn't want to leave without a picture of my baby.

There were so many people coming and going from my room. I felt like I was on display. It felt like they were sending people in to look at me just so they could say, "This woman is totally over-reacting to the pain and her dead baby." I know that's not what was happening, but it felt like it because no one was really asking any questions when they came in. They would peek in the door to observe, or they would sit down on the only other chair and listen to my pain.

I kept asking for the pictures. One of the nurses said

she would send in a doctor to talk with me about them. I knew they had them. I asked for them the day before, and the nurse said they were on the director's desk and that I could have them when I arrived that day. Since he wasn't there, no one knew about it even though I tried to explain. A different doctor came in, and I again talked him through the entire situation, all the while in horrible pain. This was true labor. Then the nurse practitioner came back in. Before she left, I'll never forget what she said to me when I asked for the pictures. She asked, "Why do you want them? Is there a fetus in there?" I would have killed her if I wasn't in so much pain.

As she left, Jay whisked me into a wheelchair. He wheeled me past the nurses' station where someone had the ultrasound pictures waiting for me. Then he ran me out the door and rushed me to the surgery center. There was no way I was going to be transported by ambulance.

If it wasn't for the pain, I would have asked Jay to drive and keep driving until we were far away from everyone and everything. "Just keep going," I would have instructed. We didn't have anything with us or any plans, but I simply wouldn't have cared. We would be alone together, able to hold each other and completely sink into our grief. We would be away from all the doc-

110

tors and nurses, suspended in time. If our baby had been older, we could go to a private place and give birth together, and then bury her like centuries before.

But there was no escaping the death within me.

I was shaken back to reality by those waves of pain and consciously aware of my journey. When I arrived at the surgery center, I got checked in. The nurse wheeled me back to an isolation room close to the OR. I was in room eight which had sliding glass doors and a curtain that was pulled closed. All the staff involved in the surgery came in and asked me my medical history. As the nurse started my IV, I finally received pain medication.

The pain relief was almost immediate. I began to feel numb. I sunk into the oversized chair as all the pain melted away. The pain medication didn't last long and I soon felt my labor pains again. Each time I felt them I asked for more medication, and it was given. As the physical pain melted away, the emotional pain became unbearable. I wanted medication that would knock me out. I found myself wishing I was already in surgery, asleep but alive; completely unaware of what I was going through. I wanted to be a drooling, bumbling mess. The kind of psychiatric patient pictured in movies who just drools and grunts because she has no idea what's going on around her.

As I continued to be prepped for surgery, I advised

them of the special procedures for collecting the baby. One of the nurses told me she knew what to do and brought in these strange tubes. All I could think about was the "test tube baby." I am not sure why I thought that, except that the tubes were large and had blue tops on them, and my baby would be put into the tube. These weren't the containers I was given to catch my baby. I knew these were specially made for the procedure.

A doctor I had never met came in to explain the procedure to me. He seemed friendly enough, and I felt like he had a good understanding of what was supposed to happen in the operating room. I didn't like the anonymity of everything. I had seen many different doctors and nurses over the last few days; there was no continuity, no time to develop a relationship. Even though I had yelled at the OBGYN director, I wanted him to do the procedure. I trusted him, despite everything. I didn't like that someone who knew nothing about me was going to take my baby from me and be part of a very intimate experience. Yet I had no choice.

The doctor explained that I would be in the OR for approximately 15 to 30 minutes while he put a speculum in my vagina. He would then insert an instrument called a dilator to dilate my cervix. The dilator would allow the doctor to insert a plastic tube that would scrape and suck contents from my uterine wall; this would ultimately remove my baby. Once I agreed that this was the procedure I was present for, I was escorted to the OR. It was OR 2.

The room was freezing. It seemed so sterile. The operating table was in the middle of the room. Everyone present was wearing the blue hair bonnets and had masks on their faces. I had no idea who they were or if I had actually met them before. I felt isolated, despite all the bodies around me. I was naked under my gown in a room that was so cold and dry. There were machines beeping, and the operating table had weird contraptions attached to it so they could spread my legs to the world. My arms would also be in the "Jesus" position as they called it. They would be tied to boards outstretched from my sides.

I was asked to lie on the table and got very scared. As much as I wanted this over, I didn't want to be there. I didn't want it to happen this way. I was on autopilot. I got up on the table and laid down. The anesthesiologist was by my head and tied my right arm down. Another nurse laid a warm blanket over my body and assured me all would be fine. I remember that no one ever said they were sorry. No one extended sympathies. They were on autopilot, too; only focused on their tasks, each choreographed perfectly. The anesthesiologist then told me she was going to administer the medication that would make me sleep. I briefly wondered if it would make me sleep permanently.

The pain of the IV in my left arm was more painful than any of my contractions. I looked up to see the anesthesiologist with a syringe full of white liquid. She counted back from ten. I only remember ten, nine, and I fell asleep.

Forty-five minutes later, I woke up. My throat was sore. I kept feeling my chest to make sure I was still breathing. I was worried I had died on the table. The surgery was only supposed to be 15 to 30 minutes, and I wasn't supposed to be intubated . . . but I was. Why?

I began asking questions. What happened? Was I still alive? Was it over? The nurse told me, "Just sleep." Even though I wasn't completely awake, the tone in her voice sounded evil. I fought hard to stay awake, but I couldn't. I felt myself drift off again. Thirty minutes later I awoke with Jay at my bedside. He told me that when the doctor went in for the procedure, our baby was still in her sac inside the birth canal. She had already passed, but they still did the D&C. I was really confused. Why would they still do the D&C if I had already passed the baby? It didn't seem right.

After another thirty minutes we were on our way home. Physically, I felt good, but I was still an emotional wreck. My bedroom was like a haunted house. It was full of reminders of my loss. My nightstand had unopened sterile containers sitting on it. The bathroom had drops of blood on the floor. There were streaks of blood on the toilet seat. Sterile containers filled with saline were lined on the side of the bathtub. I needed to get out of there. I retreated to the bed and napped.

A few hours later I was able to throw all the containers away. As hard as it was to see them, I was reluctant to discard them. They were the last pieces I had left of her . . . of my pregnancy. I cried.

That night dad took us out to eat at a Japanese steakhouse; the same place where we announced our pregnancy to Joey. It was nice going out because I felt semi-normal. What I mean is that I was out in the world, as if nothing had happened. No one knew anything about me while I was there. There was no one to argue with and no one to look at me with pity. I decided I was going to fly to my parents' house the next day with Joey. I would be away from everyone and everything. No one would know anything about me.

The next morning we went out for breakfast. I didn't eat anything. I felt so sick. I was nauseated and had a headache. I took a pain pill and felt better. After breakfast, I quickly packed myself and Joey. Joey was supposed to spend a week with my dad and mom, and

115

since I took time off work to heal it made it very easy for me to go with them. Jay took us to the airport. I know I looked like shit, but I didn't care. I just wanted to get away. I couldn't be here anymore.

My parents owned 10 acres of land in Oklahoma with a huge, ranch-style home away from suburbia. My mother owned several horses and cared for several other horses. She taught dressage classes and had jumps on her property because we used to practice hunter-jumper. My mother was usually with the horses all day, and since dad was retired he would care for Joey most of the day. This would give me time to relax and get away from my ordeal. I was looking forward to the warmth of the weather, the fresh, spring air, the trees and flowers blooming, and the quiet of the night.

Unfortunately, things were going to get much worse. Was that even possible at this point?

Chapter 12

Sunday, April 18, 2010

As soon as I got to my parents house and settled in, I laid down in bed. I wasn't feeling well at all. After having a nasty migraine and traveling all day, I needed the rest. I basically crashed on the bed last night at 8:30pm. I was nauseated and exhausted. I woke up at 2am and was extremely dizzy. I was so dizzy I thought I would pass out or fall over. I held onto the walls as I walked to the restroom. I figured I just woke up at the wrong time during REM, but a few hours later, when I got up again, the same thing happened. By 8:30am I was better, but was still lightheaded and dizzy. I decided to look up whether this was something to worry about after having surgery. It was.

I called the doctor and talked with a nurse who said I needed to go to an emergency room. By noon, we were on our way.

When we arrived I was still dizzy and nauseated. I checked in and sat in the waiting room for a bit. I told registration that I was dizzy, nauseated, and felt short of breath. Soon, I was called into triage. Mom came with me while dad and Joey waited in the waiting room. The nurse asked me questions and then took my vitals. My heart rate was too low. It was only in the upper 30's!!

I was immediately taken to a room. There was a whirlwind of people who came and left. All kinds of things were happening. I was poked, prodded, and kept on a monitor. I had an EKG, a chest x-ray, and tons of blood work. When those came back negative, I was taken for a head CT and a chest CT. The chest CT required iodine and THAT I didn't want to do, but I was worried as well. Those tests came back negative.

My mom thought it was the scopolamine patch that they placed behind my right ear following the surgery. The physician's assistant who worked with me talked with the ER doctor. They agreed the patch could be causing the problem. It certainly wasn't helping to prevent the dizziness and nausea, so they pulled it off.

After two liters of fluid I still wasn't any better. We really thought it was dehydration. That would have been an easy diagnosis, but it wasn't that simple. It was time for me to be admitted for further testing and monitoring. I certainly didn't want to pay for this but I really didn't know what was going on. Was I bleeding internally? Did I have some weird heart problem now? Should I have flown so early after surgery? Did I throw a clot?

Of course, EVERYTHING came back negative.

The hospitalist came in to talk with me about being admitted. He sat down with me and said I was depressed. I told him several times I wasn't, but he kept pressing the issue. He said that people get depressed after things like this, and that it was sad. I told him, "Yes, it's sad. But I need to move on." I could tell he didn't really believe me. He then said that depression or sadness would be totally normal for my situation.

Boy, he doesn't know the HALF of what has gone on in my life over the last four months!

I was so afraid he would schedule a psych consultation and completely ruin my chances of getting a police job. I was transferred to the 2nd floor, room 251.

I met my nurse and started to settle in for the night with my dad. I needed some stuff from home and some food, but all dad could get was food. He brought me a ham and cheese sandwich from Mazzio's. YUM, although it made me VERY nauseous that night. The nurse gave me some Zofran and that really helped. A bit later, she came in to try to give me Lovenox. I refused the meds, which I know upset them, but I am bleeding. I certainly don't need a blood thinner if I am actively bleeding. That just doesn't make any sense! I know it's supposed to help prevent blood clots since I will be in bed, but I am trying to move as best I can. I'll pass on the Lovenox, thank you!

I was supposed to be on a "vacation" away from everything that just happened, but I found myself in the hospital once again. I was really worried about what was going on with me. I knew from my experience working in a hospital that things were bad. The rush of the nurses and the number of people coming into my room, coupled with them moving me closer to the nurses' station was my first clue. As I laid on the hospital gurney, I turned to my mom and said, "Mom, something is really wrong with me." Was this a reaction to the anesthesia? Was this because I rarely took medicine so it had a stronger effect on me? Maybe they overdosed me? With all my tests coming back negative, I wondered if the problem was because my heart was broken.

By the time I made it to the hospital I was done crying. I think I was pretty much numb from the experience. *At least being admitted would give me time alone, time to think, time to process, time away from life,* I thought. It was my turn for someone to wait on me. There was some sense of relief despite the overwhelming fear and uncertainty. I knew that I wouldn't have to do anything for myself and could just grieve. I hoped people would feel sorry for me. I imagined the nurses talking about me and what I had just gone through outside my room. I imagined them gossiping at the nurses' station. It made me feel better, as if people cared. It made me feel like I wasn't totally alone in my despair.

The emergency room doctor was so insensitive. He

told me I was depressed. I am sure since all the tests came back normal, he had no idea what could be causing the problem. However, depression wouldn't cause a low heart rate, and I knew that. I felt like he was shoving the loss down my throat. What did he want from me? If I had come out and said, "Yeah, I am depressed!" What would he have done differently? The fact of the matter was it didn't matter. I was grieving, for heaven's sake! His statements really hurt.

The thought crossed my mind that my body had been through a traumatic experience, and this was its way of grieving. No one would believe me, though. I truly felt like I had no control over my body anymore. My body was trying to tell me something, but my mind wasn't listening. It took several days in the hospital for my heart rate to increase to low normal. I felt better physically, but emotionally I was still a wreck.

Chapter 13

Monday, April 19, 2010

I am scheduled for a heart ultrasound today. Things moved VERY slowly once I was admitted. The heart ultrasound was very interesting. I heard my heart and saw it on the monitor. I never thought my heart would sound like that. It wasn't anything like a baby's heartbeat. It was all swishy and whirly. They were monitoring EVERYTHING. All input AND output. I still felt sick to my stomach. I wasn't eating much. I was still spotting and passing little clots too. I want that to go away soon.

The new hospitalist and her intern came in to see me. She talked about how all my tests were coming back normal, and they weren't sure what was wrong with me. Before she left, though, I mentioned to her that I wasn't depressed. She turned to her intern and said that she was going to ask her intern if she noted my "blunted affect." The doctor believed that I was depressed just by the way I looked. Is that an official diagnosis? Seriously!! After they left, I looked up "blunted affect" on the Internet.

WHATEVER, lady!

There are all kinds of things that could make someone look that way. How about the fact that my baby died, I had surgery to remove my baby but started the miscarriage before the surgery, flew to Oklahoma to rest and relax but ended up in the hospital with bradycardia! Geez! There is NO other reason other than depression for a blunted affect?! Really? Also, I don't know you and you rubbed me the wrong way from the beginning. Sharing my history with you isn't something I want to do right now.

During the day, I was asked if I had been peeing regularly and then was asked about my bowel movements. Well, I hadn't had one since I had surgery so I knew I needed to take some-thing to go. I opted for prune juice. They brought me two cups but I made sure to start it slow. I KNEW what it could do to me. Not long after the first few sips I needed to go but I found myself shy. Mom was there and I was hooked up to a monitor. I didn't want them to know when I was pushing. Urgh! So, I waited. I waited until the urge was really strong and it would just come out and I didn't have to worry about them watching my monitor. A few hours later it happened according to plan and I felt like I unloaded the world into the toilet! It felt so good, but also, the prune juice turned much of it to liquid. GREAT! I hate diarrhea! Another issue to deal with now. The funny thing about that, though, was I almost immediately felt my heart rate go up.

30 minutes after I left the bathroom my nurse came to check on me. I asked her what my heart rate was. She went to look and came back and said my heart rate was up 10 points. I was VERY excited. I really thought that was it, but unfortunately a few hours later my heart rate returned to 38-45 bpm. My blood pressure was low and all over the place — sometimes really low like 90's over 60's and sometimes in the 100's over 80's. No matter what it was, they liked improvement.

By evening time the cardiologist came to visit. He was probably the only one who took everything into account, including my flying in from a higher altitude. I was feeling a bit better that night and he believed that my symptoms were from too much anesthesia and felt it could take 10 days to two weeks for it to completely leave my system. Great! I can't imagine feeling like this for another two weeks!! Now I am worried about my knee surgery.

After he said that my heart was fine (ejection fraction was 60%, which is good), I asked if I could be discharged. It was about 9pm. He kind of looked at me funny, but I told him I would like to leave. He said he would try to find the hospitalist but that I was already charged for the day so it didn't matter (after reading some paperwork upon discharge, that wasn't true). I told him I felt like I was taking a room that could be used for someone who was sick, but my parents told me the hospital was pretty empty. That's something I wasn't used to. At some of the hospitals I have worked for the rooms are almost always full. I couldn't help but feel I was holding up a room and keeping them from making money. I was assured that wasn't the case. Of course! If I stay all night, they can charge for more stuff!

I began to settle in for the night. At least I had my computer and my phone charger now. I really didn't want to stay overnight but my heart rate was still so low. I was still worried. I tried to make the best of it. I watched some TV, chatted with a few people and began to doze off. As soon as I began to doze, my nurse came in. "It's time for your prophylactic Lovenox." What? Seriously! I am NOT having that. I told her I didn't take it last night. She said, "You can refuse it." I said okay. Thanks for waking me up!! Urgh! Back to sleep I went. A few hours later a tech came in for my vitals and a few hours after that she returned, again, for my vitals.

As I sat in the hospital I thought to myself, *if I had just had a baby, I would be doing the same thing.* I would be recovering from my delivery. I tried to justify why I was there. Maybe I was there because my body believed that I needed to be there just like when I delivered Joey? I DID deliver a baby! I deserved this. Whatever I was attempting to rationalize wouldn't make sense to other people, so I just kept it to myself.

The doctor assigned to see patients that day had an intern with her, and they completely frustrated me. They stood at the end of my bed with their long, white lab coats and my chart, talking over me. The questions that were asked were not directed at me; they were directed at themselves. If I answered, they ignored it.

With all my tests coming out negative, I began to wonder if this was all in my head. When they mentioned the blunted affect, I almost lost it. How can you diagnose a person based on their facial expression alone? Wasn't it possible that I just didn't like them and didn't want to share my feelings with them? I consider myself a pretty open person, but I knew they weren't interested in hearing about my loss. They just wanted to stop my symptoms.

It was horrible being in the hospital, but at least I was alone. I needed to be alone to allow myself to be completely vulnerable. I needed to soak into my grief. I needed to cry, and I needed to spend as much time as possible in a "numb" state. I didn't long for my family because I wasn't lonely. I needed to be where I was. It was very helpful for me to spend this time sulking by myself and have the feeling of being waited on. If I needed anything, I usually got it. If I wanted pain medication, I received it. I didn't have to explain anything to anyone because I was alone. I could just sit there.

My family didn't intentionally leave me alone. Jason was still at home in Colorado. He wanted to come with me, but he had police recruits to train. If I had asked, I know he would have taken the time off. But I needed time away from him, as well. Jason continued to work, but he called to check on me from time to time. It was nice being so far away from him and hearing the worry and anxiety in his voice. Jason was a homebody and was with me 24/7 when he wasn't at work. While I loved him very much, it was nice to have a few moments of my own time. I didn't get this at home, so being away was a welcome relief.

Jason was also very worried that the hospital would kill me. Jason had been exposed to more natural ways of caring for ourselves and understood that doctors were just regular people who make regular mistakes, so he was worried someone would make a fatal mistake with me. I assured him I was advocating for myself like I did for my doula clients I served, but he had a hard time understanding how I could say this with confidence since I was in the hospital alone.

When I wasn't talking with Jason, I hoped he had someone to open up to about all that happened. I imagined him talking with Fazio at work. After all, we weren't talking about the loss and processing the experience together; we were only talking about what was going on with me physically at the hospital.

My mother was busy tending to the horses and my dad was busy tending to Joey. My dad would bring Joey to visit me from time to time. On his visits, Joey was very protective of me. I loved him so much, but I wanted to push him away. I just wanted to be alone. He wanted to lie with me when he was visiting. I knew he needed me and didn't understand why I was there, but I couldn't muster up the energy to mother him. Any attempt to push him away was met with guilt. I couldn't imagine what Joey was going through.

My brother and sister-in-law lived close by, but they didn't even know I was in the hospital. I wasn't on the best terms with them, so I didn't say anything to them and asked my parents to keep the situation quiet. I didn't want them to feel sorry for me or feel like I was using the situation to manipulate them into seeing me. I posted updates on Facebook and chatted with friends on the phone when I felt I had the energy. I rarely had the energy.

Getting sleep in the hospital was nearly impossible. The nurses continuously came in, disrupting every possible moment of numbness. It was as if their sole purpose was to remind me that I was there, like a little

130

brother poking his big brother. Stop touching me! Despite my familiarity with the protocol, learned after years of working in a hospital setting, I was frustrated by all the disruptions. Every time I fell asleep someone would pop in for a vitals check or for some other stupid reason.

After talking with the cardiologist I decided I wanted to go home. It became obvious there wasn't a thing they could do for me except stare at me and watch me on the monitors from the nurses' station. Even my bodily functions were being monitored and scrutinized, which felt like the ultimate invasion of privacy.

Every action I took was being judged. My nurse would look at my plate and scribble on her notepad a percentage of what was eaten. I felt like a prisoner who wasn't living up to my captor's expectations. The nurse would come in after I ate, lift the cover on the plate, and say, "25%?" She would then chart it and walk away. The tone in her voice was disapproving. Did it really matter to her if I ate?

Then there were the restroom duties. I didn't like how much blood was still coming out of me. I was required to pee in a "hat" attached to the toilet. Clots and blood filled the hat, tainting my urine. I felt embarrassed when a nurse had to look at the most intimate parts of me that are usually kept private. Every time I had to use the restroom, the same cycle of invasion and embarrassment happened. Eventually, I began dumping what was in the hat and writing the output on the board for the nurse to see. One nurse was okay with that, but some really wanted to see it. They seemed disappointed that I robbed them of their duty. It sickened me. I couldn't understand how a hospital wouldn't have a special place for women like me.

Chapter 14

Tuesday, April 20, 2010

*I awoke at 7:15am., ordered some breakfast,
and went back to sleep. 9am rolled around and I
was still sleeping. The doctor finally came in to
tell me they were going to discharge me. She
listened to my heart and left. I ate half my bagel.
I didn't feel well today, but I needed to get out of
the hospital. I was hoping that leaving would
help me feel better. It didn't.*

*The scars from this weekend are evident on
my chest. The small patches from the electrodes
that were attached to me for days have left a
sticky residue. It's awful. I miss you and I miss
being pregnant. I heard all weekend from people*

that I am depressed, or at least should be, given the circumstances. Yes, it's sad, but I don't feel well since the surgery and that really bothers me.

I just don't feel well. I honestly can't believe this is bothering me so much. You were only with us for 8 weeks, and it was such a hard 8 weeks. Not wanting you at first and then loving you so much that I was so scared to lose you — it's just unbelievable, this loss I feel. Part of it has to be that I am now considered postpartum. I'm no longer pregnant and have no baby to hold, take care of, or feed. No extra responsibility; nothing to show of my pregnancy except the sticky scars on my breasts and belly.

I'm afraid to go to sleep. My heart rate to-night is 41 and my BP is 96/65; still not good, and I am at home now. I am also weepy. I re-member this weepy feeling. It reminds me of when Joey was born. It's the same feeling. The same sense of loss only this time, things are dif-ferent. I just want to feel normal!

I was sick, and I was hurting. I wanted the world to know that my baby had died. I wanted to sleep all day. As much as I wanted to go home and feel normal, I wanted to be committed. I couldn't bear this pain. Now that I was experiencing complications, I wanted sympathy from every person that I came in contact with. I wanted to start every conversation with, "My baby just died."

I called Jason to tell him I was being discharged. He was very happy to hear I was getting out of the hospital, and he would no longer have to worry about me and what might happen while I was there. My mom came to pick me up, but I wanted a copy of my medical records and all tests before I left. I wouldn't be able to receive the medical records for a few weeks but I could pick up all my radiology tests downstairs. I filled out the paperwork needed to request my records and then my mom wheeled me down to the radiology department where I picked up the CD's that contained my CT scans and heart ultrasound. I wondered what my heart looked like on this CD. Could you see that it was broken?

I made it back to my parents' house and lay on the couch the rest of the day. When it was time for bed, I headed to the bathroom. As I undressed, I saw my body was laced with the sticky patches of electrode glue. Each patch itched, and I couldn't get the glue off my skin. I just stared at my naked body in the mirror as the shower ran and began to fill the room with warm humidity. The mirror began to fog over, but I kept staring at myself and desperately scrubbed at the patches. I wanted them gone. I wanted every reminder of this week to be gone. I felt like I was losing my mind. I was sure it was a combination of grief and hormones.

My body's creation of all these hormones was supposed to lead up to a special day. My body was perfect and knew what to do during this special day, and then suddenly, I was stripped of that experience. No baby would be delivered alive. My hormones were all out of whack, confused by the lack of a baby to nurture. It felt as if I was hit upside the head, and I didn't know which direction to go. How was I supposed to recover from this?

Chapter 15

Wednesday, April 21, 2010

Today is the day that the straw broke the camel's back. I got a call this morning from the genetics department at my HMO. Apparently, the doctor failed to submit embryonic tissue. Instead, he sent in maternal tissue for testing. Was this on purpose or was this doctor just an idiot? I don't understand how this can happen, ESPECIALLY when the doctor told Jason, while I was in recovery, that the baby was in the birth canal and he was able to collect specimens for their testing and the testing I requested. Now, I'll NEVER know what was wrong with my baby.

When I called to file a formal complaint with

my HMO, the man on the phone at the Liaison's office tried to dictate on paper what I was saying on the phone. I felt he was losing pertinent information, but I went along with him. He was ready to submit the complaint when I asked to see what he wrote. He told me that the information was internal and that I couldn't see it but that he would recap what the letter said to me. I was like, "Are you kidding me? How do I know you have all the information in the complaint?" He just kept repeating that the complaint was internal, and that I couldn't see it. I told him I didn't trust my HMO at all at this point and wanted to know how I can submit the complaint myself. He gave me the information and I began writing my letter.

After a few hours, I decided I needed a lawyer. I wanted to let them know I was serious and I want my co-pays back. I need representation. I need a lawyer to send a letter on my behalf. This is just so wrong!

I was encouraged to have the D&C in order to ensure the proper tissue was sent to the lab for testing. The doctor said he had the proper tissue for analysis. So, how is it that the wrong tissue was sent? My gut feeling is that they

didn't want me to know why this baby died be-
cause they're somehow liable. It's probably the
same reason why they didn't want me to have
the ultrasound photos. I just don't understand
why they're hiding things from me.

I became so angry when I heard what had happened. I wanted to strangle the doctor through the
phone lines. I could feel my face turning red and burn-
ing. I could feel my blood boiling. I was now stuck in
Oklahoma, and I was unable to go down to the clinic
myself and yell at this doctor in person. I was a crazy
woman who would have been flailing her arms, scream-
ing and crying about what they had done. I would have
had to be physically removed by security. How could
they do this? Who in their right mind makes this kind of
mistake? This was personal. They never wanted me to
have the testing done, so they did this on purpose; at
least, that's how I felt.

The doctor called to express his sympathy, but I
didn't want to hear it. He was negligent. I hated my insurance company for what they failed to do. They failed
in so many ways. Now I just wanted to blame them for
everything. I wanted to blame someone.

They wouldn't give me progesterone supplementation until it was too late. They didn't want to allow me

to have genetic testing done on my baby. They didn't want to give me my baby's pictures. They said I didn't need to be intubated, but I was. I didn't receive an explanation for the intubation, either. Then, I made sure to tell them over and over again how to collect the tissue. Now I find out they sent the wrong tissue?! How is this even possible? This was beginning to sound like a horror story.

I posted this on Facebook, and friends began calling me and sending me emails and messages. I was glad I had their support. At first I just wanted revenge on my insurance company, but later I changed my tune. I just didn't want other women to have to go through this experience. I didn't want another woman to lose her baby like this. My baby was supposed to be shipped to Texas for the genetic testing. Where was my baby now? I know what hospitals and labs do with "products of conception." They toss the tiny bodies into a biohazard bag and send it to incineration. For me, my "products of conception" was my baby, a human being, my daughter. She deserved more.

I remember that night I yelled at Joey. Joey wasn't listening to what I was asking him to do, and I yelled at him, ran to my room, and shut the door. I threw myself on the bed and just started crying. Joey came to the door, but I yelled at him to leave. I felt like a spoiled child who didn't get her way. It was embarrassing, yet I couldn't control myself. I didn't know what was consuming me. Was this due to hormones? I fell asleep on the bed. About forty-five minutes later, I heard a little tapping on the door and saw a note slide underneath it.

I rubbed my eyes and slowly lifted myself out of the bed. I crawled across the floor and picked up the note. It was from Joey, and it said, "Mom, I sorre." It was Joey saying he was sorry. I just broke down in tears. I opened the door and called for him. He came up and apologized again, and I just grabbed him and hugged him as tightly as I could. I cried and sobbed all over my little boy. I told him I was sorry for yelling at him and explained that I was very sad and that he didn't deserve for me to yell at him. Joey's little hands wrapped around the back of my neck and he pushed himself back, looked at me in the eyes and said, "It's okay, Mommy," and then he kissed me on the nose. I felt so blessed to have him in my life.

Chapter 16

Friday, April 23, 2010

Tomorrow Joey and I fly back to Colorado. It's hard to believe I am no longer pregnant. While I wasn't able to be happy and excited about the pregnancy because of all the complications, it is interesting how the pregnancy affected decisions I made every day. I keep thinking, 'I can't have alcohol,' and then remember that I'm not pregnant.

Every so often, I use the back of my hands to lift my boobs. I was doing that regularly to ensure they were still sore and I had SOME sort of pregnancy symptom. Now when I do this, I'm reminded that I am no longer pregnant. I am grateful they're no longer sore (as I was afraid I would make milk).

Filling the car with gas used to bother me when pregnant. I would think, "I shouldn't SMELL this . . . it's bad for the baby." Now, it doesn't matter. Even though the thought goes through my mind, it just brings sadness that I am not pregnant.

It's really hard to believe that only a few short weeks can affect so much in your life. I don't know if I can try to get pregnant again. The thought of going through something like this is so painful. I don't know if I have the strength.

Sunday, April 25, 2010

We made it back to Colorado yesterday. It was nice to come home, but everything feels different. I didn't truly notice it until I got into bed. That's when I really felt the loss. The last time I was in the bed, I had just lost the baby. It's been over a week of not being pregnant and it still feels weird. I finally got over the weirdness in Oklahoma and wasn't expecting to feel this way again.

I honestly think that it's the loss of feeling

"special" that I miss at this point. When I was pregnant, I was treated like a goddess. Jason went out of his way to do things for me. That certainly won't be the case anymore. I have returned to being "average" or the "loser" with a bum knee who can't work as a police officer. I am not so sure I WANT to work in that field anymore. I am sure it's just because of everything I have gone through over the last few months.

I am worried that Jason and I will go back to "living" together and not being a partnership. I really don't want that. I liked how he made me feel when I was pregnant. He made me feel so special and loved. That was something missing in our relationship for a long time. The baby brought that back. Will it stay? I know he's grieving as well. I am sure it will stick around for a little bit. I just don't want to end up in divorce because of this.

My life seems like a wreck right now. I am no longer pregnant and I have a bum knee. I am in limbo worse then I was before. Now I am trying to reschedule my knee surgery and I'll have to explain to my boss that I'll NEED six weeks off! I am afraid to do that. He wouldn't have hired me if that were the case.

145

I have no desire to go back to work, but I don't want to sit at home and do nothing. If I didn't work, we couldn't afford some of the things I want for the family. I need to work. I guess I am just scared to go back to work. I will feel obligated to explain to my boss what happened. Then there is the inevitable "tour" on the 2nd floor which is labor and delivery. Ugh! I will have to walk by laboring women and babies. That will be the true test.

It's already painful to see pregnant ladies, wishing I was one of them. Well, I have the power to do something about that, but I don't have the strength right now. I am still going through the issues regarding the doctor's negligence, messing up the genetics test. Hopefully we'll speak with a lawyer this week and get some of that going. I want my money back for the surgery and hospitalization.

I guess I need to try to get over all this. I need to move on. I need to find something in my life that I can do and be proud of. I need to spend more time with my family, doing things instead of just sitting around. I need to get up off my butt and exercise. That's probably the only way I'll lose any weight. In a month, I can reex-

amine if I want to have another baby.

I think the second week following the loss was the worst. I was coming out of the anesthesia, the experience, and having to return to work. My thoughts were all over the place, and I didn't know what to make of them. I didn't know how to process what I was feeling, and I was worried about my relationship with my husband returning to the struggle it was before.

We had been married for 12 years when we lost our daughter, and it was beginning to show. Getting pregnant seemed to bring our marriage new life. We were thinking about each other more, focusing on our family more, and enjoying what a pregnancy and new baby would bring. Losing our baby meant that our relationship would stagnate again, and we would be roommates as we were before the pregnancy.

Our marriage had been filled with long hours at work and I seemed to be struggling with getting Joey from one after school activity to the next. I felt like I was responsible for every detail of running the household with the exception of bringing home the larger paycheck. I was beginning to feel exhausted from working forty or more hours a week, caring for our son, cleaning the house, washing the clothes, folding the laundry, mowing the lawn, and paying the bills. I became resentful of Jason. I wanted to live his life. The way I saw things, it looked like he was going to work and enjoying life because he had less responsibility.

My resentment wore off on him and, in turn, he became resentful of me. We would get into little fights and then not talk about it. This brought on even bigger fights. Jason and I weren't touching each other, yet he still expected us to make love. It made me even more resentful. There was a time where I almost had an affair because things were getting so bad between us. I quickly ran to my priest to work out these feelings and receive religious guidance. Something needed to change and our pregnancy gave us the shift we needed.

I didn't want to return to the dullness of my marriage, and many times I wanted to jump ship. I couldn't, but I wanted to. There was no way I could bring such destruction to my son's life. I thought about finishing the basement and just living in there, but I didn't.

I knew my husband and I needed therapy. Babies don't fix a relationship, and I knew that our problems would surface again after the baby had been born anyway, so it was time to fix things. But I had no energy. I had to muddle through. I am Catholic. My marriage is Catholic. My husband is Catholic. I knew we needed to make this work. My husband and I needed to learn to communicate better. There was no solid reason to split up. We would get through this too; we always have.

Then there were the negative thoughts about pregnant women. I wondered when I would stop wishing the babies of pregnant women dead. Often I would see a pregnant woman and secretly hope that she lost her baby or that something bad would happen to her. To see a pregnant woman enjoying her pregnancy was devastating. I was jealous. I desperately wanted what she had. I wanted the belly, the glow, the attention from others. I wanted to feel the kicks of my baby, my belly growing and expanding, and I wanted the femininity that pregnancy brings.

Most of all, I wanted my baby.

I wanted to nurture my baby from conception to birth through childhood and into adulthood. I wanted another child I could raise like I was raising my son.
Because I was stripped of this experience, I wanted all pregnant women to hurt. I wanted them to experience the pain I was going through. I wanted them to know what true devastation felt like. I wanted the world around me to be in the pit of despair. I wanted no happiness around me, and I wished horrible things on pregnant women. It took months to lose that feeling. I don't think I lost that feeling until close to the New Year. It's embarrassing to admit, but I now know that

those feelings were part of the grieving process that many women who have experienced pregnancy loss go through.

Chapter 17

Monday, April 26, 2010

So, I am waiting to go to my follow-up appointment for my hospitalization. I have decided I am not going to go to a follow-up appointment for the D&C. I mean, what's the point? Unless they call and are worried about me, I don't think I should waste the time and money to go. I am so frustrated with them at this point anyway.

I don't know what to say in my appointment today. I am tired and my lungs still feel funny. I am also still upset and weepy. Last night I cried in bed . . . again. When will I feel normal? When will I be able to go to bed without feeling weepy? I am NOT a weepy person! I don't cry in front of others. I try to hide this kind of emotion. What's wrong with me? Is this depression or postpartum related?

I still have no desire to go back to work. I just don't feel ready, but I would like to go out and make some more money again. I don't want to keep being a burden to my new boss. So, I guess I will have to go back to work. I hate this!

5:30pm – I went to my doctor's appointment this morning. The appointment went normal. He was running a bit behind, so I actually had to wait. The nurse took me back. My pulse was 87! That's high for me. She took me to the room and told me they were going to do another EKG. Ugh! So, I got undressed. I was really cold and I was shaking. She came in and started to place the stickies on me. I tried really hard not to cry. I am just so tired of all this. I am ready to be normal again and not visit the doctor . . . EVER!

The nurse finished up and left. She had me get dressed and I waited for the doctor. While I waited I again tried to mask my emotions, although I really just wanted to break down and cry. Look at everything I have been through!

This is so stressful! Feel sorry for me!

The doctor came in and was his cheery self. He sat down and told me he was sorry for my loss. He then told me he thought that everything was from the anesthesia and that he's seeing another patient who is going through the same sort of complications.

He then wanted me to talk a little about what was going on. That was really hard. I tried to hide my tears. I talked a little about how the doctors thought I was depressed. He said, "Hellooo! You have every reason to be depressed!" I get that, but just because I am sad it doesn't mean I am depressed. I think we are misusing that word.

He then explained that he and his wife went through a loss a few years ago and how hard it was. I told him that I never realized I would have to experience the postpartum stuff. He said it's normal, because all the same hormones leave the body. I guess I just wished someone had warned me that all this could happen. I mean, they make it sound like you'll pass the baby and everything will go back to normal. It doesn't!

I managed to squeeze another day off out of

153

him, although it seemed like he would have written me off a few more days if I needed it. I am not sure I am emotionally ready to return to work, but I REALLY need to get back to work so I don't get fired. I am also trying to set up my knee surgery so if I don't go back to work now, it will look worse.

The funny thing is, when I called to reschedule my knee surgery they said they could get me in on Thursday! Seriously! I am not sure I am even healthy enough. My doctor said I was healthy enough to have the surgery but I might not be emotionally ready for it. I told him I would like to just get it over with. Problem is, if I have the surgery on Thursday, I will have to have general anesthesia. I believe that if I have general anesthesia, I will need to be admitted for monitoring. I asked about the spinal anesthesia. The nurse said that the doctor would have to approve it and if I were to have a spinal, I would have to wait a month because I need a morning appointment. I guess I don't mind waiting a month, but I really need to get this over with.

At this point, if I have the surgery on May 25th I won't be able to work until July. I really would like to get a police job soon.

I had a nice long lunch with Glenna today. We talked a lot about what has happened to me over the last few weeks and about her police job search, as well. Before I left, I talked a little about how I am losing faith. I really need to go see a priest but I just can't talk about all this without getting weepy. I mean, getting through my doctor's appointment without weeping was hard. So I wrote an email to Father John Paul.

Father John Paul,

I am struggling with some issues in my life and I need some help. I thought about scheduling an appointment with you but I am so weepy; I am afraid I won't get through my situation verbally. It seems that more and more obstacles are being placed in front of me and I am losing faith. I felt as if I opened myself to God's path months ago and for a while, I really felt driven by Him. But recent events have knocked me down.

I graduated from the police academy in December and was on my path to become a police officer. I was turned down by an agency but felt like it wasn't in my "plan" to work there, so I pursued other avenues. While testing for an agency, I suffered a severe injury to my knee. The injury requires surgery and basically took me out of any processes with police departments. It was unfortunate, but I scheduled my surgery and tried to stay motivated that things would work out.

Then a miracle happened. I got pregnant. I wasn't exactly happy with the timing of this miracle as I was set to have surgery and hopefully begin a police career. We also weren't trying to have a baby, but as Catholics, we were open to another child and always felt that God would bless us with another child when He felt we were ready. I hadn't been able to get pregnant without the use of fertility treatments in the past, so we felt this was a miracle from God. At this point, I felt God was trying to send me a message although I didn't know what it was. Things didn't go so well with the pregnancy. I found myself having complications and was visiting the doctors weekly for ultrasounds to ensure all was well. Despite their reassurances, I didn't feel things were going well with the pregnancy.

A few weeks ago, my feelings were con-

firmed as I learned my baby died inside me. While I wasn't that far along, I am devastated. Some people don't even believe I should be upset because the baby wasn't that old and, of course, people don't believe it was a baby. I know this baby was a life. This baby had a heart beat. I did all I could to hold on to this pregnancy. I prayed every day for this baby and prayed the Rosary almost every day for this baby. I even prayed the Rosary in church with my family and I have never done something like that. I have NEVER prayed this hard in my entire life, so I don't understand why this baby was taken from me . . . from us.

My son and husband were also devastated. I experienced complications from the procedure I had to remove my baby and was hospitalized for a few days. I only chose surgery to remove my baby in order to have the baby tested for chromosomal abnormalities, but the doctors sent in the wrong tissue for testing and I will never know. I also wanted to confirm the sex of my baby.

So many things have gone wrong. I was in church on Sunday, and I felt sick. I didn't want to participate as I normally do. I listened to your homily and just kept losing faith. Why worship God? Is it my goal to live a good life only to go to heaven and just worship God? Why is this happening? Why did I open myself up just to be hurt this way?

I apologize that this is so long. I don't know what I need. Maybe just a prayer? I know it's not for me to understand, but I am so lost and confused. I know you can't answer why. Please, pray for me.

Elizabeth

I am still drained by all this. I really just want to feel normal again. I am still running into things that I had to think about while pregnant and don't have to now. For instance, I was folding Joey's clothes last night. There were a few things I pulled out because they were getting too small for him. Instead of putting them in the basement like I had been, I remembered I could donate them. I have no reason to save his clothes now. I am no longer pregnant.

Then, we set aside a bunch of DVD's that Joey used to watch all the time. The DVD's were very scratched and unwatchable. I had plans to replace them because the new baby would watch them. Well, I don't have to worry about that anymore.

I don't have to worry about spotting anymore. I don't have to worry about drinking anymore. I don't have to worry about making sure I am eating enough protein. I don't have to worry about . . . I WISH I had all these little worries again!

I ordered a book on miscarriage. It's supposed to come on Wednesday. I can't wait for it to get here so I can start reading it and help processing some of this. I wonder if I need to seek therapy again, too. I probably should. Let's just get back to work so I can afford therapy. I am also sending the book back that I got for Joey. It's damaged, anyway, and we already read it. I am not sure how helpful it was for him.

We received sympathy cards today. I really needed that! I needed someone from the outside world to acknowledge this WAS a loss and that we ARE grieving. The cards were from the District 1 PAR team and a friend of Jason's.

I am kind of spotting today and the tops of my breasts are sore. What's up with that?

One of the more difficult aspects of losing the baby was that I didn't receive much sympathy from Jason's family. I knew my family wouldn't provide empathy or sympathy; that was just not in their nature. Even though they are Catholic, I wasn't expecting them to believe this baby was a life worth mourning. Jason's family lived so close to us. They were much closer as a family unit emotionally than my family was, so I had the expectation that they would give us some sort of support.

Unfortunately, I didn't really hear from them. I never asked Jason what he was feeling about the lack of support. I can only imagine he was disappointed as well. Still, the one person in Jason's family who I thought would reach out didn't. This was Jason's mother. My relationship with her wasn't bad, but I always wondered what she thought of me and if she really loved me like she said she did. I had hoped that this experience would bring us a bit closer because we were both women, but she had never had this kind of experience (at least she didn't express that she did). I imagined the reason she remained distant was due to her lack of understanding. Making this assumption was healing for me, because believing she didn't reach out for any other reason would have hurt more.

Jason's sister also didn't reach out. I was angered by

this. I felt like she should have reached out. I am not sure why exactly, but I really felt like this was something she would have wanted to be a part of. She fell pregnant by the end of the year, and I secretly hoped she had a miscarriage just so she would understand how I felt. I became resentful towards her. I wanted her to know how isolating it feels when the family who's close by doesn't really acknowledge the loss. It really hurt. Of course, nothing happened with her pregnancy, and I was ultimately thrilled for her. But it still hurt.

Chapter 18

Tuesday, April 27, 2010

I feel better today; almost "normal." Jason and I had a really long talk last night and I think that helped. This morning, though, I am having problems with dizziness. I was driving back from the school after dropping Joey off at BASE, and I had a weird episode where I "spaced out." It freaked me out. It was like I disappeared for a few seconds. I don't really know how to explain it. There were some distortions in my vision. My head CT came back fine, so I have no idea what's wrong.

I took a shower, and I am still feeling dizzy. My heart rate goes into the 100s when I am moving around and drops into the 70s when I am sitting. That's 15 points higher than normal. I can't call my doctor. He'll think I am crazy. Everything has come back normal, so what am I supposed to do? I am afraid to drive and just don't feel right, but can you call a doctor and say that without them thinking I am mental? I have to go to the dentist. I hope I don't get in an accident. I guess we'll see what happens.

11:45am – I went to the dentist and came home with no other issues. I have been drinking lots of water and took the rest of my thyroid medication, in case that was the problem. I have no idea what's up with me. The sad part is, I don't feel like I can call my doctor. I just don't want to be labeled as mental. Yes, I am going through a rough spot, but this doesn't feel like an emotional thing. It really feels physical. I just wish I knew what was wrong with me. A friend of mine who is a nurse thought I could be anemic or that I still have a blood clot that they haven't found. I don't know how there could be a clot since I had all kinds of blood tests and none indicated there was a clot. I had the D-dimer, a chest x-ray and CT and nothing was found.

This is so frustrating! I am now on the

phone with my HMO trying to find out where my refund is for the urgent care visit on 4-4-10. I seem to be on perpetual hold. That's also very frustrating. My HMO genetics department called me again today. I asked about the placenta, and they said that there is a placenta by 5-6 weeks. I haven't read anything that shows that, but ok, they supposedly know more. They told me that they submit placental tissue because cells are more likely to grow so they can look at the chromosomes. I asked how many tests are submitted in cases like this, and they said 10% that are submitted don't have good tissue.

Ok, GREAT! So not only am I in the 10% that had no good tissue, I am also in the 5% that miscarry after a heartbeat is seen. Gotta love statistics!!! I absolutely hate this!

It was very important for me to make sure that Jason didn't know I was hurting. I tried hard to hide the hurt when I came home. It was easy to hide the hurt in Oklahoma. I just didn't have to talk with him, and if I felt weepy I could get off the phone. At home, I had to face him. After a few days of being at home and crying as softly as I could in bed each night, I had to talk with Jason.

I talked with Jason for hours last night. We talked about how amazing Joey is and all the things that have transpired over the last few months. Jason said that he needed to learn to trust me more. He said that he believed I knew something was wrong from the very beginning. I liked hearing that. It certainly validated the feelings I had had during the pregnancy, but I am also glad that he didn't just say that something must be wrong if I am acting the way I was. That would have scared me more, and I would have been more worried. I am not sure I would have made it. I mean, if I said, "I think there is something wrong," and Jason said, "You must be right," I would have FREAKED!

Jason said that when he picked up my dad at the airport that Thursday, my dad said, "Don't make a big deal of this. You have a beautiful and wonderful son." Yes, we do, but this IS a big deal. Dad also expressed that we shouldn't have told Joey and that Joey didn't need to go through the stress. Well, how confusing would that have been for Joey? I mean, mom and dad are upset. Mom goes to the hospital for surgery. Mom comes home and then ends up in the hospital for a few days because of the surgery. Mom is still upset and crying. How is THAT not confusing? So I shouldn't have told him? It would have been harder to explain to him what happened after the fact. I am sure he would have been offended to hear, "Mommy was pregnant but the baby died and now mommy is sick. That's why mommy and daddy are upset." That sounds worse to me!

I am not upset with my dad. He's certainly entitled to his opinion; I just don't believe that we should have left Joey out of this. I wouldn't change the way I handled any of this.

So, I am on the phone with my HMO Patient Business Services now. It seems my refund was NEVER submitted to them. Okay . . . HOW INCOMPETENT ARE THESE PEOPLE?!?! It's been three weeks. I don't understand. I am so tired of this insurance dilemma.

I hope that I am okay returning to work tomorrow. I am scared to go back, but I need to go back. Work called me this morning to verify that I was on the schedule for tomorrow. That was nice of them to do. I just hope I can do this. I don't think I am ready to go back, but all I do is sit in front of the computer all day. I can't keep

167

doing that either. I need a life!

I picked up my medical records today, too. I decided I needed them for the appointment with the attorney tomorrow. Getting them was a hassle. The pathology report wasn't attached. I had to go back in to get that. The anesthesiology report wasn't in there either. I tried to get a hold of the anesthesiologist but I know that the people I talked with aren't going to pass on my message, and I will need to jump through hoops to get this report as well. Urgh!

8:00pm – I am now so upset about going to work tomorrow. I am crying, and I am angry. I don't want to work. I am not ready to leave the house. I am not ready to go back to work. Jason doesn't understand. I can tell I am being a bother to him. He gave me a big hug and asked if everything was okay. I said, "no," and just cried, but I know he thinks it's silly for me to feel this way about going back to work. All I wanted to hear from him was that I didn't have to go. I know I will go, but I just want him to say I don't have to. I mean, when I was pregnant, he said I could quit any time. Why is it that now, all of a sudden, I HAVE to go back to work?!!? Can't he just tell me I don't have to go?

Jason and I haven't been happy in our relationship for several years. Life got busy and we began to pull away from each other. Joey would always bring us back together and back to reality, but for the last few years it felt as though Jason and I were roommates and not husband and wife. I can't say for sure what marriage is supposed to feel like; I just know what my marriage was feeling like. Our pregnancy brought a fire to our lives. We had accomplished something together — something we never thought possible — and now it was gone.

Our talk that day was about everything that we had been going through and the experience of losing our baby. We hadn't really sat down and talked about things since the loss. I don't think we were ignoring it. Life was just busy again, and I was still mourning and in my shell. Jason and I had a good talk about where we wanted to go from here, and he helped me process some of the emotions inside my head. I felt much better about our marriage after this conversation, but our relationship was still weak, and I felt like we needed some intervention.

It seemed like I couldn't go anywhere without becoming emotional. It was actually quite difficult going to the dentist appointment. I didn't want to talk about what had happened with the dental assistant, but it seemed inevitable. Why? Well, as soon as I sat in the chair the dental assistant proceeded to talk with me about her trials and tribulations with her fertility or lack thereof. During a normal year, I would usually talk about my fertility issues as well and offer her support and resources; however, I didn't really care to hear her stories while she picked through my mouth.

I sat in the dentist chair, with the back all the way down. A bright light shone on my face so I couldn't see my surroundings. I felt off balance and I had to hold my mouth wide open while someone I didn't know picked through my teeth with a sharp tool. Every few seconds, the dental assistant wiped something on the paper bib that was strapped around my neck. Somehow, I began to feel very vulnerable and I realized I was holding back the tears.

The dental assistant made a comment about how my gums were bleeding quite a bit and how I needed to focus on flossing more. With that comment the emotions that were welling up inside my chest broke free. I burst into tears and said, "I have extra progesterone flowing throughout my body because my baby just died!" I couldn't see her face, but I felt her push away from my chair. Shocked at what I just said, all she could muster was, "Oh." Then she went on to explain how extra progesterone will cause excessive bleeding and that's probably the reason I was bleeding so much.

At least now she would no longer talk about her fertility issues. She finished my teeth cleaning in silence and then grabbed the dentist to check my teeth and review her work. The dentist came over and asked her questions. I heard her whisper to him that I had lost a baby recently, and I had bleeding gums. Don't they realize I am right here? If they have questions about me and what I have been through, just ask. I didn't appreciate the whispers while I was in such an odd position in a dentist chair.

Chapter 19

Wednesday, April 28, 2010

Today was my first day back to work. I was very stressed. I woke up at 3am I had to pee, but I couldn't go back to sleep. I just kept thinking about things. What am I going to tell my boss? How will I tell him I have to go out for knee surgery? How is he going to respond to me? How will I handle walking the 2nd floor (labor and delivery)?

I got out of bed at 5:45am. I hadn't been sleeping but wasn't really tired. I was nervous. I showered and went downstairs to start dinner, make my lunch, and eat breakfast. Then I got Joey up and ready for school. It kept my mind off things. While I was in the shower I came up with how I was going to tell my boss about my knee surgery. I decided I was going to say that I am better after the time off despite my hospitalization and unfortunately, this meant that I would now have to have another procedure.

That's all I was going to say — another procedure. It made it seem like it was related to this incident. He doesn't need to know what I am having done. I know it's not related, but it makes me feel better. I can have the procedure done because I am no longer pregnant . . . so it's a result of losing the baby.

I got to work with no tears. I was really surprised that I wasn't tearful at all. My boss greeted me with a hug and condolences for my loss. He kept telling me to smile. Then, he told me it was his last day. He was being removed from the hospital. Apparently, people no longer liked him there and he was being removed. GREAT! I REALLY like my boss, and I chose the hospital because I would work side-by-side with him. The ONLY positive to this was that I didn't have to feel bad about having the surgery. This new boss would just have to deal with it. I felt obligated to be there for my boss. He hand-

picked me. Now I am just some "officer" who happens to work dayshift with the new supervisor. Urgh!

The day seemed to drag on forever. I managed to walk the 2nd floor, which is the labor and delivery floor, with no problems. I even went through the Neonatal Intensive Care Unit. I really thought I would have trouble. When I came off the elevator, I took a deep breath and just started walking. I had more of a problem seeing pregnant nurses then I did seeing the babies or postpartum mothers. I am glad I didn't have to walk by a laboring woman. I walked passed a room with a new baby crying in pain. I remember thinking to myself, I am glad I don't have to deal with that. I then thought, "Joey never cried like that!"

The other area where I thought I might have issues was the bathroom — the one I normally use. It affected me more than going on the 2nd floor. As I entered the bathroom I thought, "The last time I was in here I was pregnant." Now I am not pregnant. After Joey's birth I had similar feelings about places I would visit, people I would interact with, etc. So I am not sure if it's just me or if it's part of the grief process. I

175

wanted to get in and out of the restroom as quickly as possible, so I did.

I met my new boss in the afternoon. He rubbed me the wrong way. I could tell there was tension between him and my old boss. We'll see how things go tomorrow when I work alone with him. I have a feeling I will be doing all the dirty work, and he'll be sitting in the office. I didn't tell him what happened to me. I asked my old boss if he did, and he said he didn't tell him about the incident.

I kept waiting for the day to end. My feet, legs, and hips were killing me. It was obvious that sitting for two weeks really took its toll on me. The hospital isn't that big and I was worn out by noon! I ended up taking a Motrin. I am sure the new boss didn't like the fact that I kept returning to the office to sit down for a few minutes. Oh well!

On one occasion, the new boss asked me where I came from. I had told him where and he said, "And why did you transfer here?" as if I made some mistake in transferring to a smaller hospital. I told him, "Because I was pregnant. And I didn't think it was a good place for me to be pregnant, and the supervisor there felt the same way, so I asked for a transfer." That's about all I told him regarding my situation. Let him fill in the blanks.

The day FINALLY ended and I was off to the attorney's office. It was a quick and easy drive. Jason met me there. We spent about 20 minutes with him. The attorney was very empathetic and said that we had a good case. He said that it was obvious that the doctor botched this case but that my HMO is very difficult to fight and we would need at least $20-$30,000 to fight them. My HMO fights everything, even if they know they're wrong. They want to send the message to people not to fight them. They certainly have succeeded.

The attorney tried not to downplay our case. He said that we have a "loss of chance" case. He said that we cannot get the baby back to test the baby and that's our loss. I liked the attorney.

Jason and I figured that's what we would hear. It was very comforting and helped me tremendously to hear an attorney say that I had a case. Even if I can't do anything about it, I am glad I went, and it helped me with my grieving to hear the attorney's opinion. He said the best thing we could do is send in the letter I wrote and also send in the letter to the medical licensing board. That was all he could offer.

I called my dad on the way home and let him know. He said I should find an attorney that would take our case on a contingency. He said I needed an "ambulance chaser," someone who would take a significant portion of the money won because they're greedy and will fight for more money. I am contemplating that. I don't know what I want to do at this point. I may just send in the complaint and hope for the best.

I heard back from my HMO Patient Business Services and I got my $50 back. Hopefully it's in the bank now. They cleared up the extra charges and are going to send in the refund ASAP.

I am still having bouts of dizziness. Part of me hopes that I pass out or faint at work. I don't know why. I guess I just need attention right now. I am sad. The good news is that Father John Paul moved up my appointment with him to next Monday, and my miscarriage book came. I'm reading it now.

Going back to work was extremely difficult, mostly because I felt weird being around all the people I knew. As I dressed that morning, I wondered if I would still feel my uterus when I sat down, due to my duty belt digging into my belly. I looked nearly the same as a week and a half ago, but my face was white and my body wasn't ready for the emotional toll I was about to go through. I drove into work and realized that I could no longer feel my uterus, which made me cry.

As I arrived at work, all the same people were there to greet me at shift change, but they didn't know why I was gone all this time. The only person who knew anything was my boss, and that was when I found out he was forced to leave. It was a double whammy for me. Still, what was I supposed to say when people asked where I had been?

Very few people knew I was pregnant. I felt terrified when interacting with those people. If I became weepy, I was doubly terrified about having to explain myself. If it had been appropriate to wear a sign that said, "My baby died," I would have. That way, the expression on my face, coupled with the sign, would have expressed everything.

I was quite emotional for the first few weeks back at work. Things that normally wouldn't bother me turned my world upside down. I was so sensitive that I worried I might lose my job; mostly because I was in a new job. I would snap at people for what seemed like no significant reason. I hoped things would get better for me, but

179

it seemed like there was no end in sight. I knew I needed to get through this loss, and part of my recovery was talking to a lawyer so I could get some validation for what happened with the doctors.

I wish I had sought litigation at my HMO. I still might. I want them to change several of their practices. If I was successful, many women would never experience what I went through. A lot of the pain and anxiety I experienced could have been prevented by better management of my pregnancy and the demise of the pregnancy. Having the lawyer express empathy and tell me I was right brought a sense of peace to my pain.

Chapter 20

Thursday, April 29, 2010

I have had problems with my faith. Before the pregnancy, I always felt that God had a path for me. I imagined the path was predetermined. For me, that meant God KNEW what my plan was and watched me as I either attempted to deviate (and He did something to throw me back on track) or walked in the path he set for me. Losing my baby makes me feel that all of that isn't true. Why would God set me on a path that includes such grief? God is supposed to bring life! He isn't supposed to take that new life away! That's what I struggle with. Why would God bring a new life to this world, one that would love Him and follow His ways and take all of that away? Especially in THIS world . . . in THIS time!

*I am reading my miscarriage book —
"Miscarriage, Women Sharing from the Heart"
by Marie Allen & Shelly Marks. I am pulling
lines from it that describe EXACTLY how I feel
and the way I see things. In regards to my faith,
Shelly writes it perfectly:*

*"Maybe He's just the string we hold onto to
keep from plummeting into hell. Maybe He
sometimes is a thread and sometimes a twine
and sometimes a cord or maybe He's the same
all the time and just feels different depending on
our circumstances."*

She also writes:
*"What can we do but wait and have faith?
When little children in Sunday school are taught
about faith in God, the lesson is often illustrated
by the planting of a seed with the faith that it
will become a plant. But what they don't tell you
is that some of the seeds don't make it, that
sometimes the plant never reaches the sunlight.*

182

The odds are that it will sprout and grow and blossom and flourish. But sometimes the seed never opens; sometimes it just plain dies; sometimes it gets eaten by birds."

As I read the book all kinds of things come to mind. One in particular was how I would pray at night. I remember my prayer before bed, "God, please bless this baby. Help this baby to grow strong, healthy, normal, and to full term." My prayer during Joey's pregnancy was different. "God, please bless this baby. Help this baby to grow strong and healthy and to full term." What's different? The "normal" part. I must have known there was something wrong from the very beginning!

I worry that the baby experienced a slow and agonizing death. I truly believe this baby died from a lack of hormones. I believe this baby tried so hard to grow, but that she couldn't. She didn't have the nutrients she needed. That's my fault. But I don't blame myself as some women do. I wanted the baby tested to PROVE that I was right — that this baby didn't die of chromosomal abnormalities. But we'll NEVER know because some doctor messed up and sent

183

in the wrong tissue! I wanted to know the sex of the baby. I feel the baby was a girl but don't have anything to base that on. I wanted the test so I could confirm how I felt. I had no plans to sue the doctors for not providing me with the hormones I needed. I blame them, but there was no lawsuit in mind. After talking with the attorney the other night, that wouldn't have happened, anyway.

I also realized on Wednesday that we could have gotten our baby back. The thought of this baby being placed in a biohazard bag and incinerated with other hospital trash disgusts me. Originally, we had no plans to ask for the remains. That's because the baby was going to be sent to Texas for testing. I didn't realize that the doctor had no plans to send the baby for testing! If I had known that, I would have demanded the remains. I don't know what we would have done with them. Burying them in the backyard wasn't something I wanted to do, but I certainly didn't want my baby disposed of in the trash, like she meant nothing!

Another thing that comes to mind is . . . did I ruin myself? Did I set myself up for further fertility problems because I chose the D&C? I know that I chose the D&C in order to preserve tissue for testing but it didn't work out the way I thought. The baby had already passed into the birth canal when I was under anesthesia. The doctor failed to submit the baby. The D&C was pointless. Instead, I scarred my body. How much? I don't know. I won't know until I try to get pregnant again. IF, I try to get pregnant again. I don't want to experience ANYTHING like this again. EVER!

Today at work, it became clear that we use the word 'depressed' too much. A woman came in because her mother called the police about her behavior. It was CLEAR after talking with this woman that she had every reason to be depressed. She was living in a hotel because she lost her job last summer. She lost her home . . . everything. She has no friends here. She can't find a job. She's had some horrible luck. She has EVERY reason to be depressed. She didn't act like she wanted to kill herself, but her mother seems to call the police every time she seems off or something happens, like getting a ticket. I feel for her. She seems like a normal woman who just needs a boost to get back on track. I don't know her that well, but I just didn't get the suicidal vibe from her. She seemed like a woman who was trying to reach out. She seemed like me in some ways. So, she's depressed.

Does that mean she wants to kill herself? NO! We tie depression and suicide together too much. When people have issues in their lives and can cope appropriately, why should they be labeled as depressed? Instead, when a person has issues and CAN'T cope appropriately, THEN the label applies. Then they are truly depressed and in need of help. Am I that person? Am I "depressed" because I lost my baby, my dream, a part of me? Am I coping as society deems appropriate? Should I be institutionalized?

I had a purpose in life before the pregnancy. I felt very driven and was on a good path. I was open to what God wanted for me. When I learned my baby died, all that disappeared. I lost my sense of purpose. I have no drive. I lost my desire to want to be a police officer.

I don't know what I am supposed to do now. I am just so lost! And the worst part is that I have lost the sense of time. I have no idea what day it is! I have to think VERY hard and try to consciously remember the day of the week or the date. It's not fun at all.

When I found out I was pregnant, I thought, "WOW! My body worked! I am truly a woman. It worked all on its own and I got pregnant! I made a life!" That's all gone now. My hormones weren't right. Everything about my body failed, except that I made a baby. I couldn't give this baby what she needed.

I have had some weird dreams since I lost the baby. One of the weirdest was of a funeral I was attending. The person who died looked like an acquaintance I once knew. There were white walls and a square hole in the wall on the right side. There was a black casket. Inside the casket was a blonde woman. She had long hair and I recall that she resembled my acquaintance. There were people dressed in black. They seemed to be friends of hers and they were crying and upset.

The casket was then taken to the incinerator which was the square hole on the right side of the room. They opened the door (which simply appeared) and put the casket on a mechanical concrete thing that took the casket in. When the casket went in, the person inside woke up and tried to lift the top of the casket off. Then, it shifted . . . and I was the one who was being cremated. It was REALLY weird. I woke up shortly after and thought, "You aren't supposed to have dreams about YOU dying or being dead. That means you're going to die!"

I was talking to Jason about it when I thought, "I had this dream when my baby was incinerated. That dream was about my baby." I just know it. I know I had that dream was when I was losing my baby on earth. Her physical body was gone. That's sad.

Sunday, May 02, 2010

Last night was an interesting night. I went to sleep in the spare bedroom. I didn't want to be in bed with Jason. I sent him a text message that I was going to sleep in the spare room. He told me not to do that. I told him I didn't know how to do this — meaning, our marriage. He said everything was just a misunderstanding and that he was just grouchy. I don't know. It was a rough night of text messages. He asked me to wait up for him. I tried to. I sat in the room and read my book but eventually, I fell asleep.

I heard someone in the room later. It was

Jason. He came in and saw me sleeping. He rubbed my hip and then I heard him moving things around. I had no idea what he was doing. I was out! I just knew he was there. A little while later, I felt him get into the bed with me. He curled up next to me and put his arms around me. It made me feel so good. I was so happy. We slept.

I got up around 5 realizing that Joey would be very confused to find us both in the spare bedroom, so I got up and told Jay I was moving into our bedroom. Jay went with me. Joey woke him up a bit later to make breakfast. I wanted Jay. I didn't want him to leave without us being together.

Jay got up and made Joey breakfast. He then woke me up and asked if I wanted pancakes. He was rubbing my belly and it felt really good. I told him I wanted waffles. He said he would make some for me. We just sat there. It was really nice. It turned me on big time! Joey came in and asked for eggs. I told Jason to go make him some eggs and come back up. He did. I then told him to get in the bed with me. We just sat there, holding each other. Jay was rubbing my belly. I was rubbing his back. It was nice.

Soon, we made love for the first time since the pregnancy. It was great! I know he was also being gentle, considering everything that had happened. It was very good. Afterwards, I felt sad. I remembered being pregnant and that I am no longer pregnant and that this is what started it all. I knew I wouldn't get pregnant this time because I wasn't ovulating. Still, I worried that everything would start all over again. It was also hard being away from my husband for so long in this intimate way. I had bled the entire pregnancy and wouldn't have sex even though I wanted him so badly. Pregnancy makes me very aroused. It was just sad. I missed him.

We didn't go to church. It's the first time in a long time I deliberately didn't go. I am scared to go. I am still mad too. Church just makes me want to cry. It's hard. I am glad I am meeting with Father John Paul tomorrow. I think that will really help.

Missing church on purpose made me realize I needed some religious intervention. I was turning away from God, and I felt my marriage was "on the rocks." I was so lost at this point, and I was overly sensitive to everything that was going on around me. If Jason said anything negative in the least little way, I was either upset and crying or yelling at him. I wanted to push him away and just start all over with just me and Joey. With all these feelings and the feelings I had recently, I was very happy to be meeting with Father John Paul.

I needed someone to bring me back to reality or to at least pray for me. I needed someone who I knew, without a doubt, would acknowledge my loss. I needed a priest who I had talked with before, with whom I could feel comfortable with, and who would pass no judgment.

Chapter 21

Monday, May 03, 2010

I met with Father John Paul today. I cried a lot in his office. I didn't think I would do that. I thought I was done. It was hard starting the conversation because I didn't know where to begin and I wasn't sure how much he remembered from my emails. I basically told him I didn't go to Church on Sunday because I was angry and I cry in Church. He said that leaving isn't the answer and that I need to mourn this baby. I felt like I had already mourned her, but yet there was more mourning done in his office.

It was a good talk. I think one of the most helpful things he said was that God never intended for us to die. He wanted us to live. Death isn't something he makes happen. He followed that up with statements about how we need to help ourselves here and that we can make death happen. I know he was trying hard not to say I did anything to kill my baby. I KNOW why my baby died. I might not have the test to prove it but I KNOW my baby didn't have the hormones she needed to grow and she died because of that.

He told me I had a child in heaven who was praying for me. That was also comforting. I hope it's true. I can't imagine having a child up there who I never met who's praying for me. I loved that child. I still love that child. I want her here!

He asked me to walk out with him. He had to leave and bless a new business in Parker. I walked out of the church with him. He said he would like to get to know me more and he said I could come in anytime to talk with him. As he was getting ready to get in his car, he said, "You need to name your baby." He said that I needed to pray to God for a name. I told him I already had a name. He said that I needed to pray to God to ask if the baby was a boy or girl. I told him I already knew. I said that I felt this baby was a girl and that I drew a picture of her face. I said I had a sort of vision or day dream about her and I drew her face. I said, "I know this sounds weird." He said it didn't. I didn't tell him her name. I haven't really said it out loud yet.

He then said that we needed to celebrate this baby's life. I needed to take her conception date and her death date and celebrate her life somehow. We are going to plant a tree and I am going to come up with some kind of service or family gathering to celebrate her life.

I told Jay about this on the way to dinner tonight. We were meeting his dad, my stepmother-in-law and their son for his birthday. Jay thought it was a great idea. When I told him that I named the baby, he was like, "You did?" I said, "Yes. It was on the picture I drew. You don't remember?" He said he didn't remember what it was. I had never spoken her name out loud. As we were pulling into the parking lot I said, "If we name this child, we'll NEVER be able to use this name on another child. Her name is Ruby Josephine." He said, "I could never give another child her name." I was glad that we wouldn't re-use the name.

I know that it seems weird to some people to name the baby and to celebrate the baby, but I think this is what we need to do. She had been alive. She lived in my body! She may not have been born, but she was mine, she was a part of our family. She was our daughter.

My faith was tested constantly during the pregnancy and for months following the pregnancy. I was so angry with God, and I refused to participate in anything that was related to religion or God. I no longer trusted Him, and I wanted nothing to do with Him. It was several months before I even prayed again. If I went to Church, I just sat there. I didn't listen; I tuned everything out. I was so angry that I felt like this was one way to get back at God.

It sounds so childish now, especially when I go back and read this, but it was how I felt. I didn't want Joey to grow up thinking it was okay to miss mass, so we returned to Church as quickly as we could. I am sure that Joey picked up on my non-participation. I usually sang in Church and followed along with the readings in our missal, but I couldn't bring myself to participate. I think it was close to September before I really started to get out of my "funk" and participate. While I was still hurting and felt like I had taken a direct blow from God, I was beginning to soften. I was glad I continued to go to Church. I think if I had stopped attending altogether, I would have turned farther and farther away from God, and He was a big part of my life.

Don't misunderstand me, I wasn't a "bible beater," and I don't preach the Gospel to others. In fact, I don't know much about the Gospel as I always considered myself a "cradle Catholic" (a person born into the Catholic faith as opposed to someone who converted). My husband, who converted from a Protestant faith to Catholicism, knows more about the religion. Yet, despite my lack of knowledge of the Gospel, God was a part of my daily life and I needed Him. I would see a beautiful sunset and think of God and thank Him for the splendor. My son is a huge blessing; he's my "Isaac," as Father John Paul says, so how could I be angry with God forever? I couldn't be. He brought me my beautiful and amazing son. I thank Him for it. I was resentful, but I couldn't be resentful forever. There was a reason for this loss, and while it was a reason I may not understand, I needed to learn to trust in Him. I needed to, once again, trust my path.

Chapter 22

Tuesday, May 04, 2010

So, this is the second day I spent my entire day in the ED at work. I don't want to do that. I want to continue to patrol each morning and see the same people so they get to know and like me. I was starting to go through HR and Administration each morning and now I have been stuck in the ED all day with suicidal people. My new boss seems to think that's my place, like I am his little servant. We'll see how long that lasts. I keep coming up with good ideas and he takes them and I am afraid he's going to use them without recognizing me. I need to be quiet.

There was another hard part about today that I handled surprisingly well. A call came in for a Code 3 pickup (assisting the mortuary) waiting at the main desk. My boss told me about it. I was really surprised and I asked him if he had the right location. He said that's what dispatch told him. Part of me began to think that this must involve a baby because there is no other reason I could think of for a company to come to the main desk. The main desk meant we would push a body out the main entrance.

I told my boss he should go. He said that I should go. I said, "You're just scared to go pick up the body." He said he wasn't. I could tell he wasn't going to go, so I said I would go. I left and began walking down the hall. I met the mortician at the main desk and I just KNEW it was a baby. He pulled some papers out of a purple folder labeled "babies" and asked me where he should park. He said he was picking up a baby from the laboratory.

I didn't know where he should park. I told him he could park at the docks, but that's kind of a pain. I just had him wait there. He said he would go get his box. I told him to meet me back at the main desk as I was going to check with the lab to see if they had the baby. When I went into the lab to ask, the baby wasn't there so we had to go to the 2nd floor. I had no idea where this baby would be on the 2nd floor, so I just took the mortician to the Nursery/NICU. The baby wasn't there, but a doctor called labor and delivery for us and located the baby. She took us there and we went into the soiled utility room.

People we came in contact with kept calling the baby a fetal demise, etc. The baby had a name. I saw it on the papers. "It," as the nurse referred to the baby, was a boy.

In this closet, they kept all the bio-hazard bins and trash. There was a small fridge in the room. The nurse opened the fridge and inside was a blanket. I thought, "WOW, that's a small baby." I had wondered how old the baby was. He didn't seem very heavy when the nurse picked him up. I also wondered why the baby was just wrapped in a blanket. At another hospital, they had nice little rose/paper mâché boxes to put the babies in.

The nurse kept calling the baby "it" and it started to get on my nerves. I just wanted to say, "This baby is a boy! He has a name!" I didn't. I just kept my mouth shut. The mortician put the

201

baby in the box and they sorted through paper-work. I learned that the baby was only 16 weeks. I assumed that's why the baby wasn't in a box, but I'll have to find out about that some other time.

They finished up and I escorted the mortician out. As we left he told the nurse that they do this for free for the families. He said that they bury these babies together at the cemetery and there is a little service for them. Families come to the service. When we got to the main entrance I told him that I had just talked with Father John Paul about this last night. He was kind of surprised. I said, "We lost one a few weeks ago and I'm really surprised I didn't fall apart in there." He got a sad look on his face and expressed his condolences. It was nice to get some acknowledgement of our loss.

Bringing this baby to the mortuary wasn't as painful as I had anticipated. I think what bothered me the most was the treatment of the baby. The nurse was handing the baby over to a mortuary who believes that life begins with conception. This baby was a person. The baby had a soul. The baby was a boy, and if this nurse didn't believe this baby was a person, I felt like she needed to find another job. This baby had all his fingers and toes. He looked like a human being. He was tiny, but he was a person, and she should have treated him with a bit more respect.

When I would bring deceased adults to the morgue, I always said a prayer for them on the way down. I would push them on the cart as if they were alive. If they were alive, they wouldn't be pushed head first because all they would see was me. I pushed them so they could see where they were going. I handled their bodies as carefully as I could, and I would feel bad if I accidentally let their head drop back on the cart. Did this nurse not respect life? All ages should be respected, and I was highly offended by not only her demeanor but the entire way this baby was handled.

If you remember from the journal entry, this baby was placed in a tiny refrigerator in a soiled utility room. The room reeked of afterbirth. Everything in the room was cast off. Employees would walk by the room and toss their unwanted items inside. In the back of the room, behind carts and dirty blankets, was a refrigerator I can only describe as a "dorm" fridge, something that could be picked up at Lowe's, large enough for a six pack; hardly suitable for a person's body to be laid in awaiting final disposition.

The nurse was nonchalant about the baby's death. No

sadness, just expressions that we were taking up her time and she needed to tend to live babies. When she opened the fridge and reached inside, she pulled out a blanket designed for swaddling full-term babies. The blanket was virtually weightless and, had anyone else opened the fridge, they may have pulled out the blanket and dropped the baby. The display was like a turd wrapped in toilet paper, and the nurse handled the baby as such. There was no empathy; and to call the baby "it" just made things worse for me.

I saw this baby boy's name. He deserved to be called by his name and not "it." If this were my baby, I would hope that some respect would be given, and she would be called by her name. It was almost as if the babies don't actually exist until someone calls them by name.

I read the book, "Heaven is For Real" by Todd Burpo, and one part of the book struck close to my heart. It was when the writer's son was in Heaven and met his sister who was miscarried. His mother asked what the little girl's name was and the boy replied that she didn't have a name because they didn't name her. I nearly broke down in tears when I read this part. I was so happy I had given my daughter a name. Now, I could greet her in Heaven by calling her by name and her Heavenly Father would also call her by name.

Chapter 23

Tuesday, May 25, 2010

I had my knee surgery today to correct my torn ACL. I was completely shocked and in disbelief when I was taken into the same pre-operative room and operating room used when I lost you. It was almost like a slap in the face. Once again. I became very emotional as I sat in the same chair with the doctors and nurses around me, preparing me for surgery. I miss you.

I found myself in the same surgery center, in the same room, and going into the same operating room. I don't understand how this was possible. I can only assume it was due to the size of the surgery center. I knew I would have surgery at the same center, but I never expected to be in the same pre-operative room or the same operating room. Luckily, the post-operative bay was different, although one nurse recognized me. She couldn't remember how she knew me, but I remembered her from when I lost my baby.

Recovering from this surgery was physically more difficult. Due to the anesthesia-related problems, I chose to have spinal instead of general anesthesia. This wasn't desired by the staff, but I felt I needed the safety of something that wouldn't kill me. The risk of spinal anesthesia is, of course, paralyzation. I didn't care if I ended up paralyzed. I would rather take this risk over death. Even though I would have a spinal, I wouldn't be awake for the procedure. I was given some sedation medicine that I would have to wake up from.

Due to the type of anesthesia, I would have to arrive very early and stay much later because the spinal anesthesia would take several hours to wear off. The surgery was over quickly, and I was held in the post-operative bay for many hours. Jason was able to come back and sit with me like before, but this time I had him wait longer to see me. I wanted to sleep for a while.

When I felt awake, I asked him to come back. He arrived and told me the good news. Although the news was good, I was disgruntled to hear it. When the doctor went in to repair my ACL, there wasn't anything wrong with it. The ACL had completely healed itself. There was an area on my meniscus that needed to be trimmed, because I tore it, but other than that my knee was normal. I was confused and concerned they didn't look hard enough, but the pictures the doctor brought proved all was fine. I couldn't understand how two different doctors from different clinics, one from my HMO and another from an independent facility, could get the diagnosis so wrong.

While Jason and I talked about the surgery and my recovery time, I waited for the anesthesia to wear off. After about two hours, I was finally able to move my legs, but I had to complete a task before I could leave. I needed to be able to urinate. My bladder and rear-end were still completely numb. I could feel that I needed to pee, but I couldn't pee. The nurses helped me up several times, but I still couldn't pee.

By the fourth hour, I was ready to burst. I demanded they put in a catheter to drain my bladder. They asked me to get up and try again; which I did, but failed. A catheter wasn't something I would normally ask for, but I was in pain. As soon as it was over, I felt relief; however, I still couldn't leave until they saw that I could pee.

Another two hours passed by and I began to feel my

butt again. It was so odd sitting in a chair, not feeling my butt. The feeling was really indescribable. I finally produced what the nurses wanted and was sent home. The recovery from my D&C was much faster, physically.

I found it interesting and painful that we received more support from Jason's family following my knee surgery than from the loss and devastation of our baby. My dad came down to help with Joey while I had this surgery, as well. The night following my surgery, Jason's grandparents brought us food. I remember my dad asking why they would do such a thing. I told him, "Because that's what family does, Dad." I felt sad that he didn't have this experience when he was our age. He was isolated from his family when they moved to Oklahoma and didn't have the luxury of having family close by.

I had wondered why Jason's family didn't bring anything by after we lost our baby but I wasn't going to ask. I felt that would be rude. I didn't know why they had been so distant but it was really nice to have a warm meal brought to us and helped us feel loved. The meal was absolutely delicious and I was so happy my dad could see the support we received.

Sunday, June 27, 2010

*Today I start my support group for preg-
nancy loss. I am very nervous about going but
also a bit excited. The therapist made it sound
like I might have something to offer the other
women there because I feel normal now. I don't
think I need therapy, which is part of the reason
I feel like I shouldn't go. But I'll try it just to see
what it's like.*

*It's hard to believe that I am feeling so much
better these days. It seems I have more good
days now than bad . . . and I feel guilty at times.
I really feel like I should be weeping over my
daughter. I guess I can talk about that in
therapy.*

While I felt "normal" by June, underlying grief
surfaced when I had to take a police psychological
exam for two different police departments. The psychological assessments were grueling procedures. One was
on a Tuesday, the other on a Wednesday. I wasn't concerned about taking the tests. I had taken them many
times before and although I had just experienced a traumatic event that I knew they would ask me about, I
couldn't reschedule the exams. Police agencies test on a

very strict schedule and many times the candidates who complete the process first are accepted.

I dressed in the typical business attire and prepared myself mentally for the exams. I entered the office building which was quite old. It smelled musty and had a very drab lobby. I needed to go upstairs but the elevator looked questionable, so I walked up the squeaky staircase. As I arrived at the top, I began looking for my suite number. White walls with dark brown doors lined the narrow hallway. As I arrived at the suite, I opened the door to a tiny office. There was no secretary, just a dark brown desk with a computer screen and keyboard on it. The office had more white walls with absolutely no pictures. The institutional theme was effective. I began to feel inferior.

A tall, skinny man emerged from a back office and introduced himself as the psychologist. He asked me for my driver's license and ushered me into a tiny, white room. Two walls of the room were lined with long tables with pull out chairs. There was a male in the room taking an exam. He was dressed in business attire as well. The psychologist told me to use the pencils on the table and begin with the MMPI test.

The MMPI is the Minnesota Multiphasic Personality Inventory, which was the most common test utilized for examining personality and psychopathology. This exam had approximately 567 questions. After I took this exam, I was told to start on the CPI which is the California Psychological Inventory and consisted of 434 questions. I was told not to speak to any of the other testers and when I had completed the tests, I was to set them on the desk and go out for lunch if I needed to eat. Following a brief lunch break, I would be taken into his office for an interview.

I sat down and pulled two pencils from the cup. I ensured they were sharpened and began taking the tests. The questions were similar throughout the test, but were asked in a multitude of ways. For instance, "I feel every person should vote," and "I think it's every person's right to vote," or "I hear voices," and "There are voices that tell me to do things." One of the most interesting questions on the test was "I enjoyed *Alice in Wonderland.*" Whatever that question has to do with analyzing the psyche, I am not sure. I saw *Alice in Wonderland* as a child and I loved the movie. It was a childhood fantasy to talk to animals and run around without supervision as a ten-year-old. It doesn't mean that as an adult I believe I can talk to animals. Either way, I never knew how to answer that question, I just made sure to answer it the same way every time.

The first test took a little over two hours to complete. It was draining. Once I completed the first test, I began the second. This test was very similar. It was explained to me that if I deviated in any way on my answers from the first test, I would fail. It was difficult to tell which way was up after taking the first test, but now I had to remember how I answered the first questions on the second test. I was so nervous that I would answer them differently and fail. I made sure to relax and go with my gut for each question. No one else entered the room during my test and the male who was in the room completed his tests at some point during my second test.

A few hours later, I waited for an evaluation by the psychologist. As if I wasn't drained enough! I began to feel like I was crazy! Now I was subjected to another set of personal questions by the psychologist in an arduous two hour interview. The psychologist asked me to step into his office which, thankfully, had some color; slate blue. The office was rather large with a window on one end and trinkets and plaques on another end. His desk was a massive piece of wood which he firmly placed himself behind. I saw a chair across from his desk which I assumed I would sit in but didn't until told. Any deviation from his directions could result in immediate disqualification.

He asked me to have a seat and gestured at the chair. I sat down, but didn't sit back in the chair. I sat as straight as I could with my feet firmly planted on the ground and my hands folded in my lap. He began to ask questions and I immediately felt uncomfortable. I was uncomfortable not because of the questions, but rather because of the distance between myself and his desk, which was approximately seven feet. This hardly felt like a conversational distance. I had the urge the entire time to move my chair forward but didn't.

I was basically asked to tell him everything about my life; where I came from, the traumas I experienced, drugs I may have experimented with, sexual history, financial history, etc. It was demanding and cumbersome. If I was lucky, the psychologist would tell me how I did on the tests. The tests scored me on different levels, and police agencies would only take me if I met a certain level. Anything on the low end of the spectrum would be disqualified. It was difficult to concentrate on his questions because of the distance between us and because of this one thing: I over analyzed every question he asked. After two hours, the interview was over. He completed the interview by stating he believed I would discriminate against pregnant women and babies, because I hadn't processed my experience. I HAD processed my experience!

I was shocked at what he was thinking of me. Did he think that years from now, as a police officer, I would be beating up pregnant women and using the Taser on babies? How ridiculous! I attempted to defend my position and tell him all my experiences since the miscarriage proving I had processed things, but I felt he wasn't listening. He stood up and extended his hand for a handshake. I stood up, shook his hand firmly and looked into his eyes as I thanked him for his time. He then stated, "Good luck." That was all he said. As I walked out of the room, I knew I had failed.

The difference in psychologists was prevalent that week. The exam process would be the same for Wednesday. I was dressed in the same business attire. I was mentally prepared for what the day would bring. But in the back of my mind I was concerned this would be a repeat of yesterday. The office was easier to find and felt more welcoming. The lobby to the building was open and full of glass. The halls were typical white walls with dark brown doors lining the narrow hallway, but as I entered their office, the waiting area was full of pictures of police officers and fire fighters. There was a wall displaying badges from police departments all over the State.

I was escorted to a large conference room where many males and females were taking tests around a large glass covered wood table. There was water with glasses and a large pencil holder in the middle of the table. The room was warm and had large windows that let the sunlight in on one side. It was a very bright, warm, welcoming room. I was advised not to talk with anyone and was given two tests. The MMPI again, a different version of the CPI and another test called the Myers-Briggs test which puts personalities into sixteen categories.

I began the exams and roughly five hours later I was back in the lobby awaiting my interview with the psychologist. As I perused the office pictures, badges, and plaques, an overwhelming feeling of stress and anxiety overcame me. While observing one of the plaques that mentioned the names of possible psychologists who may interview me, inscribed was the name of yesterday's psychologist.

I sat back down and began to pray. "Lord, please don't let that psychologist be the one I interview with today." I couldn't bear to go through the process again with him. After thirty minutes, a female came out of an office and called my name. I was so relieved. She introduced herself as my psychologist and I was even more relieved. This interview would be much different. She was warm and friendly and I didn't feel like I was being interviewed for a murder investigation.

She talked with me like I was a person and revealed my test results to me. She expressed empathy for my situation and I felt like she understood. She didn't focus on my childhood trauma as the psychologist from yesterday did. I felt much better and even though I might have pushed my luck in asking, I asked her if she felt as though I processed my loss. She stated she felt like I was in a good place, but the road ahead of this trauma would be filled with good days and bad days. She completely understood and I didn't feel like I failed. When the interview concluded, she shook my hand and stated she would be sending a good report to the agency. I left feeling like I accomplished something and I was extremely thankful to be blessed with a psychologist who was understanding of what happened and wouldn't use that against me.

I failed the Tuesday exam but passed the Wednesday exam. Taking those exams so close to my loss was horrible. It had only been two months. It was obvious that taking an exam following a loss would prove difficult. The same thing happened following the loss of my best friend, Charley.

I met Charley in the Marine Corps. He was a Sergeant when I had arrived in the unit and was extremely personable. A friend of Jason's, he was from Utah and had a smile that stretched a mile wide! A true cowboy in and out, he had a heart of gold. Charley was responsible for my relationship with Jason. I arrived at the band unit in late September. Jason was having a birthday party and Charley asked me to come to the party. I still had reservations because I wasn't interested in Jason but Charley had planned to put us together from the start.

Jason and I hit it off, and of course, we were married. One thing I have noticed over the years is that the friendships made in the Marine Corps, or any other service for that matter, last a lifetime. Charley and I remained friends, and he would often visit me and Jason long after we left the Marine Corps. I was pregnant with Joey when Charley married his second wife. I was unable to attend due to how far along I was, but it didn't matter, we kept in touch.

If I had problems in my marriage, I could always call Charley just to vent. Charley would always laugh at me and tell me I was "being me" and needed to look at things differently. He was the only person who could tell me I was being a "bitch" without me wanting to stab him in the throat. Sadly, Charley was killed in a motorcycle accident in 2008. It was a horrific accident, and his loss was felt throughout the world due to his status in the Marine Corps.

I had to take a psychological exam following his tragic death, which was completely devastating to me and Jason. I didn't pass that psychological exam either.

Grief affected all aspects of my life, and the testing of my psyche showed this grief. No police agency wanted a part of it. I frequently imagine Charley and Ruby playing together in Heaven. Charley would be a great resource for her. He was a loving father, husband, and friend. They're probably up there dancing and singing together.

I was both excited and scared to join a pregnancy loss support group. I didn't know what this group would bring me, or if I would benefit from it. But it turned out to be a really good experience. In an effort to provide confidentiality for the group, names have been changed. This group focused on many different types of therapies, not just talking. There was art therapy and journaling, as well as analyzing stories from the other participants as opposed to the therapist analyzing them. This was the best therapy I had ever experienced. I later returned to this therapist so she could help me process my past and grow into the person I had always known I was.

Chapter 24

October 1, 2010

The day has finally come and I don't really know how to feel. I am extremely nervous and I don't know why. Today, I will become a part of a small group of dedicated men and women to my Town. Today, I become a law enforcement officer. I am still in shock that this is real. If you were still inside me, this wouldn't be happening. I have a bunch of mixed emotions about today. I should be extremely excited but instead, I am confused, but happy.

UPDATE: The day went as expected. My family came in to celebrate with me. My dad and sister were here. It was great. I left work early and changed into my new uniform. I hadn't worn a badge yet, as this would be pinned on during the ceremony. Before I left, my co-worker asked me to come down to her office. Once there, my boss and she presented me with a card and a small plastic cake that had an electronic candle on it. When you blew on it, the candle went out. She turned it on again and laughed at me. It was really nice to be honored this way as they both supported me through this journey. They would be at Town Hall soon for the ceremony, as well.

I handpicked who I wanted to be there. My friend Tiffany, whom also shared in my loss, would be there for support and to take some photographs. I also invited my friend, Glenna. I felt bad that she hadn't been picked up by a police department, but I hoped that soon I would be at a ceremony for her. The ceremony is called a "swearing in" where I would take an oath and have my badge pinned onto my uniform.

I arrived at the Town Hall extremely nervous. I had my gun on me for the first time, but it was unloaded as I didn't have any ammunition yet. It was quite unnerving, actually, to be in a police uniform without bullets. When my lieutenant arrived, he gave me a box of ammo and I loaded in the bathroom. That also made me nervous. Several of Jason's family members were there, as was Jason, all decked out in his finest uniform. It was quite a sight.

The time came to be sworn in and I had to raise my right hand and repeat after the Town Clerk. I was so nervous I would mess up, but I didn't. I listened hard to what she said and felt I did a good job. The Chief of Police said a few words and then it was time to pin on my badge. There were sergeants and captains there, as well, and it was hard being on the spot but it was finally the day I had been longing for. It was happening!

I chose Jason to pin on my badge and we both looked at each other. I was about to tear up, but the Chief made a funny comment and I was so glad he did. I smiled with pride as I was pinned and became a police officer. After chasing this dream for over 10 years, it finally came to fruition. Pictures were taken and I signed my oath. We all went out for dinner, but dad had to leave quickly to catch a flight. It was sad to see him go, but I knew he was proud of me and I was so grateful he was able to come out. I wished my mom was there, as well.

When all was over and I was home again, I struggled with being happy and sad. I was sad that you weren't there to celebrate with me but happy for achieving the dream. I struggled to find the right feelings. It's odd when you're happy, yet sad, and then guilty about those feelings. What look are you supposed to have on your face? I tried to ignore it and just went with the flow because I knew that God had a plan for me and no matter what it was, I needed to follow that plan.

I honestly never thought this day would come. I remember feeling so sick to my stomach all morning as I waited for the afternoon swearing in to arrive. Looking back, I think I was crazy for working at my regular job that morning. I should have taken the day off and spent it with my family, who came in to celebrate, but I am a dedicated servant to the hospital and I didn't miss a beat.

My nervousness was compounded by the friends and family who would be there and the fact that I would be the center of attention. I was extremely afraid of messing something up. Would I be wearing my uniform correctly? Was my gun in the right place? Was my name tag where it was supposed to be? Did I have something on my face? Was my hair done appropriately? Was I going to repeat the oath correctly?

There was so much going through my head. To top it off, I was carrying an unloaded gun, which was extremely uncomfortable. When my ammunition arrived, I had no safe place to load. I escaped to the women's restroom in the courthouse, but this wasn't really appropriate. I was nervous I would jerk off a round, but I didn't. I knew how to handle my weapon. I grew up shooting guns, and was an excellent marksman both in the Marines and the police academy, but I was still worried I might shoot a hole through the sink.

Another issue I was dealing with was the realization that I wouldn't be here if my baby hadn't died. I would be entering my ninth month of pregnancy about this time. This thought brought a sense of sadness and melancholy to what was supposed to be my happy day. Months before, I was devastated that I was pregnant. I couldn't see beyond the pregnancy and where my career might go. All I could see and feel was my world shaken into another universe. I couldn't comprehend raising another child, yet here I was, standing before the Chief of Police, being sworn in as a police officer. I found myself confused as to what I should have been feeling.

Was I supposed to be happy or sad?

I honestly felt both, but I was more happy then any-thing, and guilt set in because of that. I really should have been mourning the loss of my daughter, but in-stead I felt like I was gloating. I felt almost ashamed to be there, but I had worked so hard and for so long. Even though these feelings were in the back of my mind, I had a wonderful day. I had my closest friends and fam-ily at this event, and it was one of the best days of my life.

I am still happy to this day that I have accomplished my dream of becoming a police officer. I couldn't have asked for a more blessed life. If another child is in store for me, I now have the opportunity to remain a police officer and stay home with that child if I left the job I have now.

Chapter 25

November 11, 2010

I have been thinking of you a lot this week. Each morning I think about you and I wonder if you would be born by now. This weekend marks a special time that I hadn't realized before. Friday is the 12th. I started to go into labor on Friday, September 12th, with Joey, which means I was in full labor on Saturday the 13th. On Sunday the 14th, Joey was born. I realized that there was a potential to have a similar situation with you. You could have been born on Sunday, November 14th, just 2 months later than Joey, albeit with a 7 year gap.

November 23, 2010

Today is your due date. Surprisingly, I am calm and I have had to purposely think of you. I find that very odd. I had planned to release some red balloons today, but Jason is working nights, so we are not together as a family to do anything. I hope to celebrate your life this weekend. I also put an intention in the prayer box for you last night. I don't know how that works, but it was the first time in my life that I had put in an intention. I don't know if I even did it right.

It's really weird thinking that I could have a new baby girl in my arms right now. I never thought that I could get pregnant on my own and now, knowing that I could have experienced this, it is very sad. It's almost disappointing, especially after having a rough day at work and wondering if I have made the right choice by becoming a supervisor. My boss is micromanaging me because of some information I passed on to a tenant and I am constantly on watch to make sure I don't say the wrong thing to the wrong person.

To be honest, I have no idea when I am saying the right or wrong things, but trying to be correct in his eyes every moment of every day is very difficult. I just don't want to be fired and have to deal with that. My instinct is to run!

A Weld County Deputy was also killed today. It's the first death in 70 years, which also worries me. Am I making the right career choice? Maybe I just need to go back to school and become a crime analyst or some other job altogether? What is my purpose in life? Should I attempt to have another baby and stay home with that baby? We don't need the money, but it's really nice being able to buy anything we want right now.

One thing I do know is that Joey wants a sibling. We were talking about you last night. I told him that you would have been born by now. He was sad and told me I wasn't pregnant and that he wished I was pregnant because he wants a brother or sister. It's really hard not having you here for him to hold and share his life. Do we have more children for the sake of our child? Will having a sibling benefit him at this age? I miss you. To top it all off, I am ovulating right now.

November 29, 2010

Tonight I went on the Now I Lay Me Down To Sleep website. It's very sad to see all the grieving parents and all the babies that have passed, but it's also healing to me. All the people on that website have something I don't have . . . a photograph. I have an ultrasound photo, but it's not a picture of you after birth.

The other day, I was on the labor and delivery floor talking about Joey. I was asked if he was my only child. This was the first time I had ever said, "He's my only living child." It felt good to say, but then I got sympathy from people on the unit which wasn't exactly what I was looking for, but it was pretty significant for me to say that.

It's getting easier and easier to call you by name, although it still feels awkward from time to time. Is that because we never got a chance to hold you? Is it because you don't seem tangible? Am I forcing myself to mourn you longer? Should I let you go and not think about you any- more? Some days I want that miracle of becoming pregnant and having a child. Other days, I don't. I really don't know who I am any-

more. Isn't that weird? I finally get all I dream of; everything I have worked towards has been achieved (although I still don't have my bachelor's degree), yet I'm telling myself that I have no idea who I am.

Who was I? This continued to be a common topic in my life. I would come to understand that this was something I wouldn't be able to solve overnight. This pregnancy loss didn't define who I was. It was just another mountain in my lifetime that I had to climb; however, the loss did change me in many ways.

Before, I had no concept of how it would feel to experience a pregnancy loss. I used to believe that women should only need to grieve if they lost their baby in the second and third trimesters. I think I felt that way because there was something physical about the loss. There would be a labor and birth of a baby. I guess I thought a first trimester baby wasn't a real baby. Even though I believed babies are babies from the moment of conception, I couldn't wrap my mind around what this truly meant until it happened to me. I couldn't comprehend the emotional side.

The emotional aspect of my loss hurt more than the physical aspect. The emotional impact seemed to last longer. I was only physically recovering for a week or so, but my emotions continued to be on the mend. My baby was a little person; only the size of a small pea. I had dreams and aspirations for her, for myself, and for my family. I thought about how we would arrange our lives when adding her to the family. Even though she wasn't any bigger than a pea, she was a person that we were excited to welcome. The physical size didn't make a difference. Now I understand that a loss is a loss no matter how early it may be.

There were times I wanted to die. I literally had lost the will to live, but I couldn't kill myself. Not every woman will feel this way, and I didn't feel it every day. However, I'll admit there were some very dark days, especially very early after my loss. I remember realizing that it was the very first time in my life when I wasn't afraid to die. A truck could have run me over, and I wouldn't worry one second about it. That wasn't normal for me, but as I pressed on through life I came out of those feelings. I didn't express much to my husband. I didn't want him to worry more than he had already. I also wasn't sure if he felt our daughter's life was worth all this pain. In the end, I was glad I never revealed those feelings to him.

It's been over a year, and I still miss her. Even though I miss her, it's not at all like it was in the first six months. I feel like I have come full circle. I am at the point in my life where I can say I have one living child without odd feelings, and I can remember my daughter and my pregnancy without experiencing an overwhelming sense of grief. I can talk about her pregnancy and her demise, and I no longer feel ashamed.

While I still can't seem to get myself to go to a baby shower, I am highly functional and don't weep at the first sign of a pregnant woman. I no longer harbor the secret wish for them or their babies to die anymore. I now realize that those hostile feelings were part of my grief process. I learned that it was very normal to feel that way.

My faith in God has resumed, but it has changed. I have returned to participating fully in mass, but as I pray there is a thought in the back of my mind that wonders if my prayers will be answered. I also pray for others more than I pray for myself. I don't believe I have complete trust in God when it comes to asking for a blessing, but I am working on the innate understanding that His plan isn't something I'll fully grasp. I still follow the adage that "everything happens for a reason," although when that was said to me during the early stages of my loss I became angry. Even so, I believe there was a reason for this loss.

I believe I was meant to endure this to develop a stronger understanding of life, faith, and love. I took for granted the intricacy of conception and pregnancy. I had the naïve belief that pregnancy was normal and that there wasn't a thing to worry about. This experience has tainted those thoughts and feelings. I now understand that many things can go wrong at many different points during pregnancy, and although that seems negative it's brought me so much power and understanding of the true miracle I have in my son.

I believe that this experience has allowed me to know and understand there is a greater purpose in life even if I can't see it. I am not meant to know my path. I'll trust my intuition and follow my heart. I'll allow myself to feel and express my grief. I'll open the door to growth and opportunity. As an unknown author wrote, "An Angel in the book of life wrote down our baby's birth, and whispered as she closed the book . . . Too beautiful for earth." Maybe our daughter was "Too beautiful for Earth?" God didn't take my baby from me, but rather had a different path for her. She wasn't meant to breathe life on this Earth.

This experience has also changed me, ultimately designing me to be a more loving and compassionate person. Joey's birth blossomed me into being a mother and advocate for pregnant women. This loss developed a passion in me to help others through their experiences of loss. When I was going through my certification process to become a doula many years ago, part of the required readings were books on miscarriage, stillbirth, and infant loss. I had no concept or understanding of how powerful these books were. I read them as stories and although sad, I shrugged my shoulders to them as if the losses were no big deal. After all, this had never happened to me, nor would it (in my naïve world).

I now understand that women grieve the loss of their babies no matter how young. I have complete compassion for this experience. It has not scarred me; it has etched a memory and experience into my soul forever.

Writing this book has been extremely helpful and healing for me. It has allowed something good to come from my most devastating experience. I never in a million years fathomed that I would be led down the path of writing this book. I have been through some extremely painful experiences in my life, but this was by far the most excruciating. I truly believe I was meant to endure this loss so this book could be created. I have a voice and I can give other women who have experienced this, their voice. At the time of publication, there wasn't a single book that existed of this magnitude.

Beyond grief lies hope. I have hope. I have emerged from the death of my daughter a stronger, more compassionate person. She has helped me open doors to vulnerability that never before existed. She's helped me heal not only from her loss, but from other traumas that have happened throughout my life. A loss like this is difficult, but in the end we will ALL make it through this.

The journey was difficult and wrought with anguish. I believe what made this so difficult wasn't only the combination of emotional and physical pain, but the loss of a different future. As the lawyer we consulted stated; we experienced "A loss of chance."

Helpful Information

Hospitals and Miscarriage

I will say that many hospitals miss the mark when it comes to pregnancy loss. The hospital I work for actually has a very good program, although I don't believe it's complete for mothers who lose their babies in the first trimester and early second trimester, mostly because these losses occur in the emergency department. If you do have your miscarriage in the labor and delivery unit, you'll probably receive much more care and understanding for your loss and your baby will be treated as a true person. The hospital I work for has nice paper mâché memorial boxes in which they place babies who have passed. In most cases, the length of gestation doesn't matter, although the youngest baby I have seen placed in one of these boxes was 12 weeks.

There are so many more resources for women who lose their babies at birth or in their late second trimester and third trimester. I often wonder if that's due to the fact that our state doesn't recognize a fetus until 20 weeks. I have talked with certain directors at my hospital to see what programs they offer for early losses. It seems there are no true programs in place. They give out a packet of information. Handing someone who has just experienced a loss a packet of resources doesn't really help. What is needed is physical and emotional support. I have placed several organizations in the resources section at the end of this book that can help you receive the physical and emotional support you need. It would be a dream of mine to have this book given to every woman who suffers through a first trimester loss.

One of the easiest options the hospital can put in place is to provide a bereavement nurse who will provide comfort. Even if the nurse doesn't specialize in pregnancy loss, a nurse who can give support no matter how early the loss can make a huge difference in a woman's grief experience. Many women will feel that their four week-old embryo is a child to mourn and will grieve that loss as if the child were living.

Also, when I became pregnant I instantly began calling my baby a baby. I didn't refer to my baby as an embryo or a fetus. But when I miscarried the terms used

236

by the doctors and nurses were cold and un-human. "Your embryo stopped growing at eight weeks." My embryo? When I hear the term embryo, I often think of an egg yolk. When does an embryo become a fetus? According to the Mayo Clinic, an embryo becomes a fetus at eleven weeks gestation, or nine weeks after conception. So, are fetuses babies? It didn't matter what term the medical staff used, I lost a baby, not an embryo.

Hearing these terms may be quite difficult for you. Even though I work in a hospital and am familiar with medical terms, it still hurts to hear my baby referred to as an embryo, fetus, tissue, and mostly, products of conception. I know they're not doing this to cause hurt or pain; they're only utilizing the terms assigned to them. My pathology report describes my daughter as "an apparent embryo measuring approximately 1cm." That "embryo's," name was Ruby Josephine.

Miscarriage at Home

Since my miscarriage, I have come across a common question regarding natural miscarriage. It seems that many people want to know how long miscarrying naturally would take. I too wanted to know because I didn't feel like I could wait weeks for my miscarriage to occur. The fact is that there is no way to know how long the miscarriage process will take. Some women can stay pregnant with a passed baby for several weeks or months before their body releases it, while other women's body's release it very soon. My miscarriage began once I stopped taking the progesterone supplementation but this won't happen for everyone.

Many women will choose to have their miscarriage naturally. A miscarriage typically starts with spotting and leads to cramping and heavy bleeding. In addition, women report clots (large and small) as well as gray tissue; some have even reported seeing their tiny babies. One woman I spoke with explained that she felt her eleven week baby slip through her vagina and into the toilet. She retrieved her baby from the bloody toilet and buried the baby in her backyard.

If you choose to miscarry at home, you could ask the doctor's office to provide you with a "hat" that fits over the toilet seat. It will allow the urine to flow through but will catch your baby. These "hats" are often used with people who have kidney stones. Seeing your tiny baby can be healing for you, but it can also be traumatic. I wasn't sure if I could handle seeing my baby or any part of my baby. Having someone with you during the miscarriage who can support you through this can be very beneficial. Most of the women I have talked with had a sense that "this was it" and there was no question whether or not they were losing their babies.

I was also offered a drug to assist me with timing my miscarriage. The drug was called Misoprostal (also known as Cytotec or Prostaglandin E1). A miscarriage will typically start within a few hours after administering the drug. I was well aware of Cytotec through my years working as a doula, and I was afraid of this drug. Cytotec is a drug used to prevent stomach ulcers in people who are taking drugs that irritate their stomach lining such as Aspirin and other pain medications. It was also discovered to cause miscarriage and pre-term labor so it began being used "off-label" to assist with labor induction and planned pregnancy termination.

Unfortunately, it was discovered that women and babies were dying with the use of Cytotec for labor induction. The manufacturer put out a warning for all doctors to stop using this drug in pregnant women due to the risk of hemorrhage and uterine rupture which could ultimately cause the death of the baby or mother, or loss of uterus (See Reference Materials). Cytotec causes the uterus to contract. In many cases, it causes uterine hyper-stimulation, which causes the hemorrhage or rupture.

Knowing how dangerous this drug could be, I didn't want to use it for my miscarriage. In addition, I had read stories online from women who used it, describing their miscarriages as excruciating. I was already in pain both physically and emotionally. I didn't want to further that pain. Still, many women choose this method for miscarriage and that's okay. Just be educated on the use of this drug and have a plan in place if you begin to hemorrhage such as calling 911 or driving emergently to the nearest hospital.

Choosing to have a miscarriage at home may be a good option for you. I was given the option to have my miscarriage at home but chose to have a D&C. My journal explains how I felt about miscarrying naturally. I wanted to do this for me and for my baby, but there were many reasons why I ended up having the D&C. Whether you choose to pass your baby naturally or with the use of a drug, be prepared by having someone available to you for physical and emotional support, as well as in case of an emergency. Don't do this alone.

Emotional Expression

I am not a crier. I tend to hold my emotions in; but I needed to cry with this loss. It was important to my healing process. It seemed to make even more of an impact to cry with someone else who was also crying. Connecting with someone who really seemed to understand, or who even went through the same horrible loss, was healing for me. I only had one friend, Tiffany, who went through such a loss. Tiffany provided love and support at exactly the moment I needed it. I had one other friend, Glenna, who had never been pregnant whom I could lean on. It was amazing to discover Glenna could support me. She hadn't experienced pregnancy or pregnancy loss but was able to understand what I was experiencing and knew what I needed to experience.

Grief is grief and she knew how to support someone through grief. Tiffany provided the same comfort, arriving at my house and allowing me to cry with her. Having that kind of support system during your grieving process is important.

I had many other friends that were there but most didn't know what to say and remained silent. There will also be people who won't understand. There will be people who leave. These people either don't know what to say or are too uncomfortable with the topic. I recommend that you focus on the friends who are there for you. You need support, and you can't be worried about a friend being upset with you because you're grieving. Your grief won't look like mine and won't look like anyone else's for that matter. There is no right way to grieve. Just do it. You need to.

241

Friends and Family

I'll say straight out that you won't be able to lean on every friend, sister, mother, or family member. This event won't affect them the same way it's affected you. I quickly learned who I could lean on. I was surprised by some of the people who ended up being there for me, and some of the people who I expected to be there, weren't. I lost a very dear friend during my journey.

When I became pregnant I turned to her for support, because I knew I could rely on her and she wanted this for me just as much as I did. I met her while working as a professional birth assistant. In the beginning I mentored her, but as the years went on we became business partners and she would mentor me in different aspects of the birth world. When she learned I was miscarrying, she sent me a text message that was shocking to me. While I understood why she sent it later and where she was coming from, her statement was ultimately the demise of our relationship.

As I lay on my bed, bleeding and in pain, she told me I had killed my baby due to too many ultrasounds. To hear that I may have caused this was even more painful than the physical pain I was in. It took me months to process what she said and why she said it. I truly believe now that it wasn't meant to be mean, but at the time, it hurt so deeply — especially coming from her. I have forgiven her for the statement, but I know that I cannot return to that friendship. I lost the ability to lean on her during an integral part of my loss.

My friend, Tiffany, was there for me every step of the way. She had experienced her own losses and was still in pain over those losses. She was easy for me to lean on. However, I caution you when turning to other mothers who've experienced a loss. Not all of them feel pain for their loss, and some won't share their pain with you. I have found that mothers who are willing to share their pain and allow you into their lives to lean on will make themselves known to you.

Another friend who was there for me was Glenna. I found her to be the most surprising out of all my friends and family. I mentioned the reason for this in the previous section. Glenna's support was unbelievable, and I'll never forget it. While she wasn't there every second of every day to pick me up, she knew the best thing she could do for me was to make sure I knew she was there if I needed her.

Every morning, like clockwork, I would receive a text message from her. They were short, simple messages, "How are you today?" "Thinking of you." "Hope things are going ok," etc. It helped me tremendously to know she was thinking of me and that she was there if I needed her. She helped me and my family in so many ways, but this was the most helpful way. What made it even better was that if I didn't respond to her text messages, she would still send one the next day. I didn't have to respond. She was there, and that was all we both needed. She knew that in time I would be able to respond. When I did, she responded back and was caring about what I experienced.

Unfortunately, my mother wasn't the person I could lean on the most. In fact, I didn't lean on her much at all. I knew my mother experienced a loss during her first pregnancy, but she never talked with me about it. I heard bits and pieces about that loss from Jason, because my dad shared certain parts of her story with him. I didn't feel like her loss was something she mourned the way I did. I could be wrong, but when I was in Oklahoma after the loss, she didn't talk with me about her loss, and I felt like she was only nurturing me to ensure I would come out of the grief process. She didn't want to grieve with me. Maybe she was uncomfortable? Maybe she DID grieve the loss of her first baby? Maybe she just didn't know what to say? It was a similar issue with my sisters.

I had to "unfriend" my older sister on Facebook. She was my confidant at other periods in my life, but I quickly learned that during my grieving process she couldn't be there for me. She got so upset with me when I didn't tell her I was out of the hospital, and she started saying nasty things about me on Facebook. I didn't need that, so I let her go. We're still close, and we're once again "Facebook friends," but during that time I couldn't have her around. I needed to focus on me and what I was going through. I needed to allow myself to sink into my grief without worrying if I was keeping her in the loop enough.

My little sister sent her condolences, but I knew and understood this was something beyond her experiences. At that time, I was unable to share with my brother and my in-law's. It became apparent to me that Jason's family didn't know how to reach out to me. I chose not to share too much with them as a result. That became more difficult as time went on, especially when my sister-in-law became pregnant.

It was difficult not to take the silence from friends and family personally. Death makes people un-comfortable. The death of a child, infant, or unborn baby makes people even more uncomfortable. This experience is taboo and is often kept hidden.

One of my neighbors sent me a message offering condolences. I didn't know how she found out that I lost my baby, but she sent me a message the day of my D&C. The message following her condolences stated,

"I told my daughter and she didn't realize this was something that could even happen."

Pregnancy is supposed to be easy and many people cannot comprehend the death of an unborn baby. Her daughter was ten at the time, but I know she isn't alone in her surprise. Many adults cannot process this type of loss.

Because of this, try not to take their silence or inappropriate comments personally. Be prepared to be assertive and set boundaries. It's okay to express what you need and what you don't need. If someone makes an inappropriate comment, it's okay to tell them. Most people aren't trying to be malicious or hurtful; they just don't know what to do.

Saying It

I lost a baby. My baby died. My daughter passed away. I have one living child. It's hard at first. Sometimes it's still awkward, but it's true. Being able to acknowledge what happened and to say it aloud makes it more real and easier to accept. For me, this was an important part of my grieving process. How can one grieve something if they can't acknowledge they have something to grieve about? I saw a bumper sticker that helped me understand this more clearly. The bumper sticker said, "If it's not a life, you're not pregnant!" I had never seen it displayed this way before. It helped. When I run into people who think my grief over this loss isn't valid, I remember that bumper sticker.

If you're afraid to tell people what happened, try not to be. It can be very healing for you to say it out loud. It felt weird in the beginning, but the more I said it, the easier it became. If you don't feel like you need to say it, that's okay, too. What's important is that you do what feels right for you. I wasn't sure what was right, but I felt the need to say it out loud, so I did.

I am blessed with the most wonderful and loving son in the entire world. His compassion and empathy for me and our family is the most amazing testimony of God's work. Joey has always wanted a sibling. He has been asking for one since he was about three. I know he would make the best big brother around. This was evidenced by how he stuck up for his dead sister not too long after our loss. It struck me how a child can often stand up and speak the truth much easier than us adults. He had been picked on by kids at school after the loss because he would say he had a baby sister but he could not produce her. The following story is a depiction of his thought process at that time:

Joey and I were at the grocery store. We

247

made it to the checkout line, and Joey had a drink clasped in his hand, saying he wanted to keep it with him and have in the car. Joey turned on his charm and asked very politely if the clerk would kindly scan his drink and return it to him. I saw this clerk all the time, and she thought Joey was adorable.

She asked me, "Is he your only one?" Rather than explaining the complicating and difficult situation I was enduring at the time, I replied, "Yeah." She replied, "One's enough." I was a bit offended by her statement, but I just brushed it off. Little did I know, Joey was about to give her a lesson in life.

He said, "Well actually, I have a baby sister, but she died." The look on the clerk's face was one of fear. She stepped back, her eyes dilated, and the look of surprise washed her face. It was obvious she had no idea what to say, and I could tell she was embarrassed. Her jaw dropped, and I didn't know if she wanted to start crying, hide, or both. I knew her statement wasn't malicious or intended to make me feel as if Joey was a handful. Even though I was a bit offended by her comment, I felt now as if I needed to save her from something. I exclaimed that everything was okay and that she didn't need to worry. I hoped that she would finish checking my groceries and bag them so I could duck out of the store as quickly as possible. Why should I have felt this way? Why should Joey not have been able to tell his story from his perspective? He wanted a sibling badly, and this was the only way he could share her. I told Jason about this when I got home, and he told me to tell Joey not to say things like that again. I told him that I couldn't take this away from Joey. It was obvious how Joey felt, and I wasn't going to downplay his loss. To this day, I haven't told Joey to keep Ruby quiet. Joey knew Ruby was real. He saw what I went through. He experienced it too. He needed this.

Situations like this WILL happen. It's unavoidable. It's not ideal to feel like you have to comfort someone who only needs comforting because they're uncomfortable. Nothing is worse than comforting someone when you're the one that needs comforting. There is no way around it, so just do the best you can. Practice saying it:

My name is Elizabeth and my daughter died April 13, 2010. I miss her every day.

Announcing the Baby

This is a very touchy subject for some, but if you feel you need to do this, do it! I wasn't sure what the right thing to do was. One day, when I was processing the loss with my priest, he made the statement that I should honor the baby. This child deserved a moment in time. After talking with him, I was convinced that I needed to put together an announcement.

My big question was how?

A standard baby announcement wouldn't work. I knew this would have to be quite different than anything I had ever seen before.

I searched the Internet but didn't find much regarding early pregnancy loss announcements. I searched a few bereavement sites, but there wasn't anything applicable to my situation. Some sites had jewelry, mementos that the mother can wear, or gifts people can give bereaved parents. I didn't want any of those things.

After much searching, I soon realized that I would have to develop something on my own. I was fully prepared to do so since I had experience assisting families with creating DVD's to announce their new baby's birth.

I had also dabbled in photography after my son was born. Since I had all the programs I needed on my computer, I began my work. I wanted to put the picture I had drawn of my daughter on the announcement, but it had gone missing. I attempted to re-draw the picture, but it didn't come out the same. Since my artistic ability was lacking, I began a search on the Internet for a baby's face.

All I wanted was a face of a baby. Every face I kept coming across seemed happy, bubbly, sleeping, etc. I wanted a specific look. The look of the baby had to be right, and after much searching, I got lucky. I found a picture where the face was unrecognizable, which was perfect. There was no way to distinguish the sex or any features of the baby. The other important part was that the baby's face was looking down and away. It was as if the only features you could see were the eye lashes.

I chose the picture. Unfortunately, I couldn't find the copyright owner so my mother hand sketched a baby face for the cover of this book. Then I needed to come up with a statement. I needed something that explained the situation and wasn't too much like an obituary. I searched memorial sites again for a prayer or a nice statement about the loss. After much searching, I was successful. I put that on the photo card and finished it with a few final touches. I didn't want to discount my religion despite being upset with God and hurt over this loss. I put a white cross in the corner of the card. The final piece of the card had to be something that was baby-like, but not too much. How was that even possible? I needed a good representation. My intuition was telling me I needed something that flies, something carefree, something that would basically represent my daughter: A dragonfly. I searched the Internet up and down for the right dragonfly. I eventually found one in the perfect shape and colors and placed it on the photo card. It was now complete.

After it felt done, I did a little research on what the dragonfly symbolized and the meanings I found seemed perfect. I love my intuition! I try to trust it and follow it with everything I do. The dragonfly symbolized her flight. It was a strong one because she was strong. She fought to stay alive, despite not having sufficient hormones on her journey. She tried, but her strength gave out. Dragonflies have strong wings, so this was a perfect representation of her. The dragonfly also symbolizes an opening of the mind. This process had certainly opened my mind, but I now saw my daughter as a dragonfly who could give me strength and share an experience that I never knew I was meant to have. To whom would I distribute the announcement? I didn't want to send it to all my friends and family — only the ones I knew would be supportive. I settled on my immediate family, my husband's immediate family, a close friend, and my priest. I had to order them through

252

a website and pick them up at my local Target. I can only imagine what the person printing the photo card was thinking. I rushed to get them. I packed each announcement, a copy of a picture my son drew for his sister, and a few words written by my husband and me into the envelope. I sent them off in the mail.

I had doubts that my family would be accepting of the announcement. Even though they were Catholic, it seemed like this would make them uncomfortable. I didn't care. I needed to do this. I also explained myself in the letter with my son's picture and a few words. I regret doing that. I didn't need to justify why we made an announcement and named the baby. A loss is a loss, and I shouldn't have worried about how they might feel or take the announcement.

We didn't tell anyone the baby's name until the announcement reached them. My husband's family called, and a few really liked the sentiment. I didn't hear a peep out of mine. It was expected, but there was still hope they might say something. When they didn't and a few days had passed, I sent my mom an email asking what she thought of the baby's name. She said, "The middle name was my mom's middle name. What does the first name mean?" Really? I explained to her how we came up with her first name but I was surprised that was all she got from the announcement. I sensed she was upset that we named our dead daughter after her mother. Again, I didn't care. I needed this, and my daughter deserved this.

There are a lot of different ways to announce and honor the baby. I recently asked my husband to add a coconut to his arm tattoo. This tattoo is elaborate, and it represents our family. We both got tattoos while on vacation in Hawaii several years ago. I wasn't a "tattoo person," but I guess I was going through a semi-midlife crisis at the time (motorcycle riding and scuba diving). His tattoo has three palm trees on a beach with Diamondhead in the background and a sunset. It's a beautiful, hand drawn piece of art.

The three palm trees are different sizes. The smallest tree represents Joey, the next largest tree represents me, and the largest represents Jason, who is the head of the household. What could we put on this tattoo to represent Ruby? I could ask to add another tree, but a coconut seemed more appropriate. I only asked him to put it on his tree though. To the date of this writing, I didn't explain to him why I wanted him to do this. The coconut would represent our daughter.

In addition, I want to hang her announcement in the house. She needs more of a presence around here. I don't want to forget her. I want people to know she existed. I think it's a simple thing to do. I'll find a proper frame.

If this doesn't sound like something you'd like to do, you could also send out email announcements, put an obituary in the paper, give small gifts of remembrance such as birth stone jewelry, buy a bracelet, necklace, ring, or memorialize your baby in the other ways mentioned below.

Baby Samples, Magazines, and More.

Remember when you signed up online to receive free magazines, formula samples, and other baby items? If you don't, you'll certainly remember when they come pouring in six, twelve, and eighteen months after the loss of your baby. Some women don't have to sign up online because their doctor's office will sign them up at the first prenatal visit. Unfortunately, many of these companies share your information, so the news spreads and you soon find yourself with stacks of samples and magazines in addition to an email box full of mail telling you all about the development of your baby next week.

These can be hurtful reminders of what you lost. If you remember where you signed up, you can return to the website and unsubscribe, but if you don't, it may be best to enlist your partner, friend, or family member to assist you in calling the companies or fishing through your emails to unsubscribe to all these reminders.

Just this month I received a post card in the mail from my local grocery store advising me that I am eligible for a free "baby's first cake" with the purchase of a quarter sheet cake for my baby's first birthday. Even though I have gone through extensive therapy, this was still a painful reminder of what I lost. My daughter would be turning one next month. In addition, I received several packets from a very popular life insurance provider over the last year, with quotes for me to sign my new baby up for life insurance.

I also went through an old email account and began deleting the 1300 messages that have been piling up in the box. I typically use that email account for signing up online for things services where I know I'll receive junk mail. I needed the email in order to work with a support group for Asherman's Syndrome. As I deleted the emails ten at a time, I watched my pregnancy in reverse. "What to expect at your delivery." DELETE. "Week 36: Your baby's development." DELETE. "Week 28: Your baby's development." DELETE.

How depressing!

Another aspect to remember will be the hospital bills that come pouring in several weeks and even months after the loss. If your husband or partner can pay those up front for you, this may help alleviate reliving those memories. You can also contact your insurance companies or the doctors and ask them to send the bills addressed to your husband only.

Should I Name my Baby?

Just like announcing the baby, naming the baby may not be the right thing for you. Some women feel called to name their baby. I did. At the time, though, I didn't know if it was right. My priest helped assist me with my decision to name our daughter. It doesn't matter how far along you were when you experienced your loss. Again, the baby is a baby to you. You had hopes and dreams and aspirations for this baby. Some of you may have already been picking out names. From the first day we found out, we were talking about names. The baby was real for us. The only names we could come up with were girl names, which was similar to when we could only come up with boy names during my son's pregnancy.

We had basically decided on a name for a girl that first night. That became her name. Some of you may have been so early in your pregnancy that it would be impossible to know the sex. If you feel compelled to name your baby, you can either choose a name that's not gender specific or you can choose a name based on

257

the gender your intuition has prompted you toward.

I am a firm believer in trusting your intuition. This baby was a girl from the moment she was conceived. Her energy was within me, and I felt her presence. Despite not having mortal confirmation, I had spiritual confirmation through prayer and intuition. Jason didn't doubt these feelings and he also felt we had a daughter. With all this evidence, we felt we needed to name her. She deserved a name.

When I met with my priest, he also advised us to name her. I found it interesting that when he mentioned this, I had already felt like it was something we needed to do. I just needed someone to push us in that direction. It felt strange, don't get me wrong, but once I named her I felt so much better.

Funeral or Memorial Service

There are few hospitals that discuss the option of having a funeral with families who have experienced a first trimester or early second trimester loss. It's not widely known that this is a possibility for such a young baby. Many of you who read this book will have already missed the opportunity if it wasn't already afforded to you. I first learned of funerals or burials for early miscarriage while working at my job not long after my loss.

The Catholic diocese has certain plots where babies can be buried together when they're born too soon. Each baby's name can be placed on a stone or memorial at the cemetery. I found out about this option too late for me to be able to do this for my baby. My baby was incinerated with hospital garbage, which wasn't something I chose. I am not against cremation. Many miscarried babies are cremated. I just wish I had a choice. It hurts to know that I could have given more to my baby.

If you still have time, remember that you can honor your baby this way by asking about communal burial or cremation. Your hospital may not know of any services, but you can call local funeral homes or your church. You don't have to be Catholic. Many Protestant faiths and other religions have these resources and can provide assistance.

Even if you don't have your baby's body, just like we didn't, you can still have a memorial service. My husband and I talked about putting a service together at our home, but in the end we chose to send an announcement, instead. A memorial can be appropriate and very healing. If this is something you desire, you can either send out invitations or call your friends and family members and ask them to come to the service.

The service might look similar to a wake. There

could be flowers and a table displaying your baby's name, pictures of your pregnancy, ultrasound pictures, and other items you may have to remember your baby. A sign-in book can also be bought and you could add this to your memory box. Prayers or thoughts/poems could be read to those who attend and there could be an opportunity for people to come forward and talk. A memorial service doesn't have to look like anything specific, so trust what feels right to you.

Rituals

I knew I wanted to do something special on her due date, but what? Release balloons? Send flowers down a stream? Light a candle? Flowers? A day off from work spent in nature? These were some of the things I had seen done by others when searching the Internet. I really liked the idea of releasing balloons. Unfortunately, her due date was Thanksgiving. I know that due dates are just an estimation, and rarely are babies born on their due date, but for her to be due on or around Thanksgiving was quite depressing. I actually dreaded her due date.

Thanksgiving is always a happy time with our family. We spend the day cooking and talking. Her due date was on a day that was typically reserved for joy, but this time I would be sad over her loss and I knew no one would mention the significance of the day. I realize now that we will always remember her on Thanksgiving, but that first Thanksgiving on her due date was met with sadness and grief.

For many, it can be healing to do something to honor your experience and your baby on your baby's expected due date or other dates that seem significant. There are many options. Some people plant a tree. We wanted to plant a tree on the anniversary date of the pregnancy. We researched trees, contacted a few landscape companies, and contacted a past doula client who was a landscaper. We decided to go with my past client because it would be more intimate and personal. Unfortunately, the whole idea fell through. Also, the tree I wanted wasn't good for our climate.

Some people also get a memorial plaque made, a birthstone, or donate to a charitable organization. There are also organizations that put together bereavement walks for pregnancy loss. I am fortunate enough to live in a state that has such an organization. They focus on bereavement care, resources, and support for those touched by different types of loss, including miscarriage, stillbirth, or neonatal death. I actually stumbled across a bereavement walk last year when I was on police duty.

261

There is an angel statue off a trail near a park not too far from our house. One day I was patrolling the trail and saw a line of bags with candles in them lighting the way to the angel statue. We pulled over and talked with one of the organizers. She explained that there was a ceremony that night at a local church for bereaved parents of babies. She told us they would walk from the church to the statue for a small memorial. I became tearful that night and wished I wasn't on duty so I could attend. I talked with the organizer about my loss, and we soon left. In researching the walk this year, I came across a similar one that happens every October. Some M.E.N.D. (Mommies Enduring Neonatal Death) chapters also host these walks. I encourage you to look for these types of events in your area.

Baby Book

I would like to create a scrapbook dedicated to my daughter which would hold all my mementos, pictures, writings, and work I did in therapy related to the loss. I found an example of one while researching memorials for miscarriage.

Unfortunately, I couldn't find it again.

So far I haven't yet had the energy to scrapbook a baby book, so all my stuff is still piled in the office.

Some of the items I had put in the scrapbook include: my positive pregnancy test, lab results, ultrasound photos, hospital band from my D&C, my complete journal, pictures I drew, poems, work from therapy, the birth announcement, pictures my son drew for his sister, and the sympathy cards we received.

A baby book or a memory box is a great way to keep all your important mementos together. For those who are reading this and experienced a later loss, pictures from your labor, birth, or NICU could be placed in the book or box, along with a lock of hair. Other suitable items might be pictures or cards from your baby shower, the outfit you were planning on bringing your baby home in, your baby's band, your hospital band, and handprints and/or footprints. Other items from the hospital, such as a baby blanket, can also be placed in the book or box.

There is also a wonderful organization called, Now I Lay Me Down To Sleep (www.nilmdts.org) which provides free photography services following your loss. The photographers are volunteers that come to your hospital room and take pictures of you, your family, and your baby for you to treasure. This is a great organization that will tailor their services to you. If your baby is too small or has a visual defect, the photographers will assist you with taking pictures of just hands or feet in order to preserve memories you can cherish forever. Some hospitals dress babies who pass. You can place your baby's clothes in the book or box.

Whatever you choose, it's important that it feels right to you. If you're reading this as you're experiencing your loss, keep in mind you might not be in an emotional state to make these decisions, and that's okay. If you didn't get any of these mementos or you weren't given options, this may be difficult for you. This is where I recommend journaling and placing some of your journal pages in your baby book. If you can put on paper all your experiences, you'll be able to revisit those later on.

You won't go back in the baby book for positive memories; you'll be visiting the book to remember your child. There is no right or wrong way. Everyone will use their baby book differently. I hope to get all my daughter's items in a scrapbook before this memoir is published.

Mother's Day

Sunday, May 9, 2010

It's Mother's Day. Am I a mother of one or a mother of two? It's a sad day today. I don't want

264

to do anything, but I know we'll celebrate. This is usually the SECOND BEST day for me all year (next to Christmas) but I am sad and I don't want to celebrate. No one in Jason's family has really acknowledged our loss. It's as if this baby never existed in their eyes. That's probably the hardest part about today, since we'll spend the day with them.

I am a mother of two. I need to remember that!

It's hard for most women to believe they're a mother if they have no living children. After all, society doesn't really recognize motherhood until you have the trophy (a living child) to show for it. I am blessed with a living son, but what about women who haven't yet been able to bring a living child into this world? Aren't they mothers? I believe the answer is yes. You conceived a child in your womb and did all the right things for that child. Many of you prayed for that child's health, and many of you may feel guilty thinking that you did something that may have caused this. Your baby didn't die because of anything you did. It still doesn't change the fact that you had a child, and you lost that child. I believe you're a mother from the moment that baby was conceived. I believe that you deserve to celebrate

Mother's Day in whatever way feels right for you.

Children and Miscarriage

Some of my journal entries contain stories about my son's experiences. This was a very difficult time for him, and he experienced the loss just as much as we did. Again, as we look back on this experience, my husband and I believe that Joey knew she had passed. There was no explanation for his vomiting. It came on when I had to go to the doctor and disappeared as we came home. It was like he knew and was in shock that his dream just collapsed. We think his intuition was in high gear and that he was connected to this pregnancy spiritually.

If you told your children about your pregnancy and experienced the loss with them, a book for children on miscarriage exists and can be helpful. There are several on the market and I list them in the resource section at the end of this book. I bought a book for my son. It was actually purchased before I lost the baby. I felt I needed a book in case of a miscarriage. It was just one of the many "feelings" I had with this pregnancy. The book I bought had great ratings, but it was geared more towards later pregnancy loss. Keep in mind, this will be very difficult to read to your children. As much as I wanted to read this to my son as quickly as possible, it took me a while to muster up the courage to read it without bawling.

If you didn't share your pregnancy with your children, they'll sense that something is wrong no matter how hard you try to hide your feelings and emotions. While this isn't something I personally did, I know that no matter how hard I tried to shelter my son from the feelings I was experiencing, it was impossible. I was in pain both physically and emotionally. He knew it, and it scared him. He had never seen me like this before, and he needed to know what was wrong with his mother.

As you read in my journal, it wasn't necessarily my choice to tell my son that I was pregnant. My husband wanted to experience all of this as a family, no matter what happened. I wasn't completely on board at the time, but I understood where he was coming from. I probably should have trusted my intuition, but how were we going to keep this from him when everyone else knew? It would have been impossible. I knew it would be hard when I lost the baby, but I felt I could depend on my husband to help with the situation.

Children also grieve. While I knew my son was upset over the loss, I couldn't fully comprehend what he was going through or what his grief would look like. As much as we talked about it, I am not sure how much he understood. Looking back, I believe his grief came in the form of stomachaches and disagreements at school. There were many times Joey would come home upset that his friends told him he didn't have a real sister because she wasn't alive. It was so hurtful to him, and the only solace I could offer him was telling him that we don't see Jesus and he's no longer alive, but that doesn't mean we don't believe in Him. I think that helped him realize that even though he can't physically touch his sister, see her, or talk to her, it doesn't mean she never existed.

One day, several months after the loss, our daughter was mentioned. Joey came out and said that her death was his fault. I was in complete shock. I had to talk with my therapist about this because I was so concerned. My husband and I both explained to him immediately that this wasn't his fault, but it was still hard to hear him say that he felt guilty about it. We had been told by the school psychiatrist that he kept talking about a sister, but she was unaware that we had a daughter. It was a difficult conversation to have with her, but after explaining what happened, I think she tried to work with Joey to process the loss. The conversation we had with him that night seemed to help him because he didn't have many of the same issues after that.

Grief in children comes in many forms. I looked

desperately to find group therapy or a therapist that could help us with him, but everything was geared toward infant loss. The miscarriage book I bought wasn't much comfort for Joey. The mother depicted in the book was just too far along in her pregnancy.

My son is the most important person in my life and such a blessing. I felt guilty for putting him through this experience, and I felt like I needed to move on from this loss quickly so he could have his mother back. I realize now this wasn't possible, but at the time it felt like the logical solution. If you're having intense feelings of guilt, try to take some time out for your children . . . but understand you're not superwoman and this will be a small blip on their screen years later. Do your best to help them understand what you're experiencing and talk with them about their experience. It's been a year and a half since we lost our baby, and Joey doesn't seem scarred from this loss.

Your husband or boyfriend

While women experience an emotional *and* physical loss, men will only experience the emotional loss. They won't experience the cramps, feeling that their bodies failed, leaky breasts, or the return of menstruation; but your partner will most likely experience some level of emotional grief. He'll watch his partner go through an experience he may not fully understand, and it may make him uncomfortable to realize he cannot take away any of the emotional or physical pain. He may suppress his grief in order to support you.

You may also get frustrated with him because he may not seem to grieve. It's very common for men to grieve differently than women or for people who didn't experience the loss on a physical level to grieve differently. Men tend to grieve in a more private way. It can also be very difficult for you if your man isn't attached to the pregnancy. For an early loss, the only attachment your partner may have is an ultrasound picture. He didn't experience food cravings, nausea, or a growing belly with kicks and punches. You may feel at times like you're grieving alone.

Check in with him. Ask him questions and let him know you need support. Make sure you tell him specific ways he can support you. Tell him you need him to hold you, talk with you, or ask you questions about what you're experiencing. He needs to know how to help you. He may have never been through this before and he most likely cannot read your mind. He'll need guidance on how to help you.

My husband was devastated with this loss. He was attached to this baby from the moment he saw the positive pregnancy test. I didn't realize how devastating it was for him until months after our loss. I didn't check in on my husband as often as I should have. I have a journal entry written months after our loss:

September 12, 2010

> *We cried over you today. Daddy and I were having a deep conversation about things that are going on in our relationship, and it came up that I would be nice and big and pregnant right now. I just started weeping and your daddy started crying. He talked about how he never got to process this, and how he had no one to talk with. I felt so bad. He had to be strong for me and Joey, and he never got to grieve you.*
>
> *I asked him what you looked like, and he said you had brown hair. I then had him read a poem I wrote that talked about what you looked like, and we realized that we both have seen you. Thank you for revealing yourself to us. It's so hard knowing you're not with us and will never be born. I love you and I don't even know you.*

This was the first time I realized my husband needed to grieve. While I was the one who carried our baby and physically experienced the loss, he also had an emotional attachment. I truly believe he was attached so quickly because he already had a son. I don't recall him being emotionally attached to Joey at such an early stage in that pregnancy.

We understood what it meant to be parents. We understood what it meant to bring another child into this world, and we wanted it to be right from the start. Jason had the same thoughts and feelings I did. He named the baby from day one. It was silly for me to think he wasn't in as much pain as I was. This won't be the same for every partner.

The poem I wrote was very powerful. I wrote this one day as I was trying to remember a day dream I had while I was patrolling the hospital in the vehicle. In addition to drawing a picture of her face, I needed to put words to what I saw in that dream. I had to share this with my husband when I saw how much pain was still in him.

I saw you in a dream,
My girl with auburn hair.
Your eyes were blue
And skin, fair.
You laughed so sweet
As you looked at me

On a warm summer day
On the green grass.
The gentle wind blew your hair
While you squinted your eyes.
Some day we'll finally meet.

This poem was healing to all of us. It helped us understand that we both dreamed about her. It provided a bit of closure we didn't think possible.

Going Back to Work

All I can say here is "Milk it!" Milk it as many days as possible because you need this time. If it doesn't feel right and you're not ready, don't go back to work if you can afford the time off. You need to take the time to not only heal physically, but also emotionally. Remember, every pregnant woman, regardless of whether or not her baby is born alive or dead, needs time to heal. Your body has produced hormones and adjusted in ways we don't fully understand or know. It can't go back to pre-pregnancy state immediately.

Some women may produce milk. That will need to be handled, as well. I was fortunate and didn't produce any, but many women do, especially if it's a later loss. Some women donate their breast milk, in their baby's

273

honor, to a milk bank. I knew that I would donate my milk if I produced any (I donated milk after my son was born). But I was relieved that I didn't. I couldn't imagine going back to work and having to pump or bind my breasts. I suggest you take at least a week off so you can ensure that you don't have to suffer through this.

Many work situations are not accommodating to regular crying spells, so I recommend that you wait to go back until you're past the early weepy stages of postpartum hormonal changes and grief. If you aren't feeling better in two to three weeks, I recommend you seek some professional help. Looking back at my story, I think I should have probably seen a therapist shortly after the loss. Know that grief is hard, and it can take a long time to feel "normal" again.

Another reason to take time off is to work out how you'll deal with any questions or hurtful comments from coworkers. It may be helpful for you to send out a mass email to your co-workers explaining what happened and give them ideas on what they can say to you to support you through this loss. You can also send this email to friends and family. It's perfectly acceptable for you to explain in the email exactly what they should and shouldn't say to you. I have learned that people don't want to be hurtful and are often trying to be helpful. Sometimes they miss the mark.

It's okay for you to educate people about how their comments can be more helpful. You can be very specific and let people know that they can say comments such as, "I am so sorry for your loss. I am here for you." Let them know you may just need to talk or cry and it's okay that they just listen and not try to fix things. You can also tell them in the email what not to say, such as, "You can always have another." "It was God's plan." "It's nature's way of dealing with a sick baby." "You already have a child and should feel blessed." Sometimes people say those things, trying to make you feel better. In the end, those comments usually do more harm than good. It's appropriate for you to let people know that.

Remember that these comments aren't meant to be hurtful. Situations like this make others uncomfortable. Miscarriage is very common, but we usually have to grieve in the silence of our own homes. We can help others understand this type of loss by talking about it and telling them how to respond. It won't only help them help us, but if they know anyone else who experiences a miscarriage, they'll know what to say.

Journaling

This book wouldn't have been possible without my

275

journal entries. Writing down my thoughts was extremely healing. I go back and read my entries from time to time to help me see how far I have come. It was a long journey, and my journal is still very important to me.

My journal was a release. I knew it was something I could run to. My words would flow faster in my mind than I could type them, and I type fast. My journal became my mate. Not all of my journal entries are a part of this book. Some of them weren't related to the loss, and some of them were too intimate to allow the world to read. Journaling helped me tremendously through this loss.

Journaling can help in so many ways. If you're currently experiencing a pregnancy that may end in loss, I recommend you journal. You can journal each day, several times a day, or even only once a week. It doesn't matter how often you journal. When you have to deal with something difficult, your journal can be a companion to you. There is no right or wrong way to journal. You can journal about the happy moments as well as the sad ones. You can journal about what your baby may look like. You can even draw your baby and make that part of your journal. Your journal can be filled with letters to your baby or you can talk about the medical aspects of your loss and any other struggles you're having.

Your journal can hold whatever needs to be released. Journaling also helps to take some of the pressure off your partner. While your partner most likely wants to help you, he may not want to hear the story over and over again. I found that was the case with my husband. I don't think he ever came out and said, "Stop talking about it," because he always seemed to lend me an ear; but I know the repetition was just as painful for him. My journal helped me to talk about it over and over again, no matter how many times I needed to, in order to process what I was feeling.

I found typing was easier for me than writing, but if you prefer you can write in a nice journal book or you can grab any old notebook. Go with what feels good to you. Some of my journals were on paper, but most of my journals were typed.

Therapy

It can be very helpful to find a good therapist or support group. I was fortunate enough to see a posting on Facebook for a free miscarriage support group. I was weary at first, because the group was going to start approximately three months after my loss and I didn't think I really needed the therapy so long after the loss. Boy, was I wrong!

277

The therapy consisted of just a few of us with two therapists in the beginning; one had experienced a loss. She ended up having to drop out of the group later due to a work schedule change. That was kind of tough as we really liked her and wanted to hear her stories to help us through. This therapy was different from anything I had experienced before. We did a lot of talking and crying, as well as art therapy, journaling, and connecting. It was very interesting and healing.

August 22, 2010

Therapy is going really well. I didn't think I needed it, but after the first day I realized I did. Today I needed to bring in an interesting assignment. The therapist isn't like any therapist I have seen before. She really makes me step out of my shell and express myself in different ways. Today, I had to bring in a poem. My family and I went camping and while I was driving home from the campsite, I stopped at the top of the mountain pass and began to weep.

I was weeping for several reasons but mostly because my eyes had been opened and I felt extremely close to God at that moment. The wind was blowing "just right," the temperature was perfect, the sun was to my back, and I had the best view of the mountains and the lake below where I had just spent a nice weekend with my family. As I approached the summit, I kept feeling "nudged," so I pulled over and stood facing west. I stood on the side of the mountain road, spread out my arms as if to fly, and took in a deep breath. I could smell the pine trees, the clean, crisp air, and I turned my face to the sky as if to summon the Lord into my soul.

I knew I would never feel this way again, so when my therapist asked me to write down those feelings and express them to the group I was both excited, yet scared. This kind of expression wasn't something I was used to.

The Mountain

I had a moment with God today on top of the mountain, although I didn't feel high enough. I wanted to go up more and more. I was on top of the world. If one could truly feel happiness, this is what it would feel like. Free, open, bright, floating, gentle wind in my face. True Peace. I didn't think I could describe what I felt today, but that was it. The world was quiet, cool, yet warm. I was in the sky. As high as my car could take me that day. I was alone. At peace with life. It was amazing. If I could feel that way every day, I would. If I could reach that limit every day, I would. Tears rolled down my face in pure happiness and joy for what was revealed to me.

I used to have dreams of flying. That's what it felt like. I spread my arms to feel the wind. I stood on the edge of the dirt and soaked it in. I was at peace. I was away from all that ails me. The other side of the mountain would reveal life again. While I couldn't wait to reach the summit and bask in its beauty, I knew I had to return to life and the other side of the mountain would bring that. The happiness seemed to subside.

August 29, 2010

My assignment for today was very painful. I have never before been pushed to these depths of my imagination, and while I enjoy it, this also scares me to death. Today I had to write a letter from my daughter to me. This is part of the healing process, but it was very difficult to do. It also brought on so much pain because I'll never hold my daughter. I'll never really know her and

280

the hole in my heart for her will never be filled.

Mom,

I will see you when you get here. Don't cry. You tried your best to bring me to your world and I love you for that. This was meant to be this way and I am okay with this. I hope you're learning what was intended. You have the daughter you were meant to have even though I am not with you physically. I am here for you in spirit, watching and learning all you hoped of me. I have no regrets, you shouldn't either. I am strong, like you.

Until We Meet,
Ruby

The group wasn't large. There was supposed to be four of us, but it ended up just being another mom and me. We liked the smallness of the group because we got lots of time to work with the therapist and learn about each other. Genevieve had lost two babies years ago. Seeing how much pain she still had inside really helped me. It validated my own grief. Knowing it was okay to be in that much pain years later was healing for me.

Genevieve probably wouldn't have been in as much pain if she had had the opportunity to process her grief years ago.

Genevieve was also Catholic. I think this allowed us to connect on a deeper level. Genevieve named the baby she lost the second time, but had not named the baby she lost first as a teenager. Hearing her talk about that loss was amazing to me. She was so young, but really wanted her baby. It was devastating to her to lose her daughter. She had no support, as her family was quite upset about the pregnancy. The only person she could go to for support was her boyfriend, who later became her husband. She was very isolated, but somehow managed to make it through. She was very healing for me.

Below is an assignment we needed to complete in therapy. Our therapist asked us to complete the sentence, "What I lost…"

What I lost was a dream. A dream I had dreamed of for years. That dream was crushed not only for me, but for my family. I lost the pregnancy. Just me. No one else. She was mine and I lost her. I wonder what she thinks of me, what they think of me.

I had really wanted my friend, Tiffany, to attend the

sessions because I knew that she still carried pain from her losses years ago. I could never convince her to go, but I still hope she does one day. Genevieve changed dramatically during our ten week sessions. She arrived in tears, nearly unable to speak about her loss. Towards the end, she was talking about her loss with no tears and had even named her baby! Her transformation really helped me to see that it was okay to move forward.

At the end of the sessions, we gave each other gifts and the therapist gave us each a gift. The gift I received from Genevieve was handmade and absolutely amazing. I had a difficult time picking something out for her, but I knew I wanted to get her some jewelry. I took my son with me when I picked out her jewelry. Joey wanted to get her a butterfly, but I felt a turtle was more appropriate because turtles represent wisdom. After hearing her story and learning about all she wanted for her daughter as a teenager, I believed she was truly wise. After our group had ended, we parted ways, and Genevieve and I remain Facebook friends.

A few months after the group ended, I returned to the therapist who facilitated the pregnancy loss group. I began to see her on a regular basis to help me "find myself." My loss still comes up during the sessions, especially when I talk about my desire to have another baby, a desire which comes and goes.

Postpartum

You were pregnant. Now you're not. It doesn't matter if you had a living baby or a dead one, your body will be in a postpartum state. I gained 15 pounds in the seven months following my loss. I still haven't lost the weight. It's frustrating. I realize that some of the weight gain had to do with the fact that I had no desire to function normally. I had no desire to work out or eat right. I was depressed. I tried to focus on all the good things that were happening to me; and I had really good things happening. It still didn't change the fact that I was no longer with child.

I am learning to love my body, and hopefully I will lose the weight once I become familiar with my new look. I try to focus on the good parts of my body, even though for months I would stare in the mirror and call myself "ugly." This is normal. You may or may not experience this, but if you do, it's normal. Believe me. Ask my amazing therapist!

The same warnings for postpartum depression apply after a pregnancy loss. In fact, 12% of women will experience depression and 20% will experience a combination of depression and grief (you can study the reference material for this data at the end of the book). Grief is normal and you may experience all the stages of grief — denial, anger, guilt, depression, and acceptance.

If you're feeling sad and weepy for longer than two weeks, are feeling no desire to live, have had thoughts of suicide, or have planned your suicide, seek treatment immediately. If you experience the last two symptoms, you need to check into an emergency department immediately. Grief will last a long time, but you shouldn't be weepy every hour of every day. The weepiness should gradually improve. Even if you spent 5 minutes less weeping today versus yesterday, that's improvement. You will get better. If you don't, you need to seek help from a professional.

You may bleed or spot for few weeks, you may experience cramping, your period may not resume for several weeks and you may produce milk or experience breast engorgement (see reference materials). You also have pregnancy hormones in your body that could take months to get out of your system.

Due to your body changing from a pregnant state to a non-pregnant state, you may not want to have sex for a long time. Talk with your partner about this. It's just like after you have a baby. Your vagina may hurt, you may be bleeding, and you may feel this could lead you down the road to another failed pregnancy. Your hormones will be off kilter because they are going back to a pre-pregnancy state. This is all normal. If it's debilitating for you, contact your doctor or OBGYN. It shouldn't be years before you feel like having sex again, but a few months isn't atypical.

Mysterious Illnesses

My sister-in-law is pregnant. She's actually due on Joey's birthday, so she's pregnant at the same time I was eight years ago. I love her, support her, and will help her as best I can; but I absolutely could NOT go to her baby shower. I couldn't watch everyone gawk over her while she received presents and everyone ogle her belly. The excitement of her impending birth would be too much for me to handle. I was jealous. I wanted everything that she was going to get. I wanted everyone to gawk and ogle over me, but my baby died. My daughter would have been eight months old and I would have brought her with me to the baby shower. Instead, I was still mourning what I had lost over a year later and I didn't know how to express this to my sister-in-law or the family. After all, they had been so quiet following our loss; I didn't know what they would think if I told them I was still mourning over a year later.

I was so torn over how to tell her and her mom (who happened to be living with me at the time) that I made myself sick. I got strep throat. It was the WORST strep throat I have ever had in my entire life! Yes, we can make ourselves sick with REAL illnesses! I didn't truly believe it until I experienced it personally. No one else in my family got sick and I wasn't exposed to the illness. I am sure I made it happen!

The strep throat was a blessing in disguise because I didn't have to go to the baby shower. In fact, I couldn't. I was so worn out from the illness that I couldn't physically move and I didn't want to expose anyone else, especially my pregnant sister-in-law. This gave me a legitimate excuse not to go, but I didn't want them to think I wasn't going because I was sick. I wanted everyone to know that I couldn't emotionally handle going. I never told them I wasn't planning on going; I merely kept it a secret in hopes I would be able to muster an excuse not to go.

For over a year, I struggled with dizziness and heart rate issues. I attribute this to my loss as well. I believe my heart was actually broken. It was physically broken by the loss of my daughter. There is no way to prove this, but the fact that all my tests came out normal leads me to believe that there was an emotional cause for my slow heart rate and dizziness.

I have run the gamut of testing, from neurology to cardiology, from ENT to acupuncture and chiropractics.

So far, there is no other way to explain this mysterious medical condition. I was emotionally destroyed after my daughter's loss, and a hole exists in my heart for my daughter. When I look back at my heart issues following my D&C, I am not fully convinced that the cause was anesthesia. I believe that my heart no longer wanted to function after I lost my daughter. It simply lost the will to beat appropriately.

My physical condition has improved after writing this book. The act of writing and finally having a voice about my loss has been very healing. I believe we can manifest real illnesses connected to grief, abuse, and other psychological issues. I see mental health patients on a daily basis who have these same experiences. How do we stop these manifestations that are completely real? A good therapist who helped me learn new skills for coping and living seemed to help me.

Pregnancy Following a Loss

At the time I began writing this book, I was torn regarding having another baby. However, my husband and I decided to try to conceive again. Even so, the practical side of me doesn't want to have another baby while the emotional part of me is really drawn to having another child. My decision was a difficult one.

If Joey was younger, it would have been a much easier decision to make. Now that he's so self-sufficient, it's difficult to want to go back to depending on family and friends to watch a baby in order to have any time alone. I have learned how important my alone time is. Plus, I work now and I am not so certain I would want to go back to staying home with a baby. This is purely a selfish decision, but I am excited to be on this journey.

Another aspect of trying again is the fear of enduring another miscarriage. I feel more prepared than ever if I had to face the experience again, but my heart hurt so deeply the first time that I fear for the pain of a second loss. I truly believe that a second loss would guarantee Joey to be an only child.

There are many factors that must be taken into consideration when deciding the right time to try again. Ensure you're talking with your doctor about the best time to try to conceive. I am not a medical professional, but most doctors recommend a few cycles pass before attempting another pregnancy. While you may be physically ready to conceive, you must also be emotionally prepared for the journey.

Many women will go on to have another baby. Unfortunately, I have the added difficulty of infertility. Some women will also struggle with infertility. I am working closely with my doctor and therapist to ensure all areas of my care are covered. It's been almost two years since my baby died and physically, I am ready. I feel I have come far emotionally regarding my loss, but it's been years since I had to struggle with the emotional and physical aspects of fertility treatments, monitoring, and the financial burden.

Having another baby won't take away the sadness or grief you experience because of your loss. Some women may actually feel more guilt because they conceived again. This guilt may stem from feeling like you haven't grieved the loss completely and are attempting to replace the baby, or because you conceived too soon. These are all normal feelings. You can write a letter to your new baby or a letter to the baby you lost and explain your feelings. This can be very therapeutic. Putting your thoughts on paper and re-reading them really helps make sense of them. Writing this book has been very therapeutic for me, as it has placed all my emotions and feelings in one space, and I can return to them any time I want.

You may also have doubts about your healthcare provider or insurance company. I certainly have doubts about the treatment I'll receive when I conceive again. I don't trust many of the OBGYN's that work for this HMO, and I have had to advocate for everything I wanted or thought I needed. But I have been doing my research on home birth as well as doctors within this HMO that will serve my needs.

It will be important for you to find a provider you can trust. If you have the option of "doctor shopping," find a doctor you trust and reveal your prior loss(es) to them. This will build not only trust in their abilities but will build trust in yourself that you can find a care provider for you and your baby.

You may also worry about this pregnancy. I know that I will experience anxiety over another pregnancy, and I am concerned that this worry could be passed onto the baby I am carrying. Try to focus on all the positive things that are taking place and acknowledge the wonder and awe of this current pregnancy. You may find it helpful to share the news of your pregnancy with trusted friends and family members so you have people you can count on for support when you're overly anxious.

Even though I knew my pregnancy would end early, I still wanted people to know what I was going through and to have a few close friends to lean on. If I were to get pregnant again, I would still announce my pregnancy early. I feel the only thing I would do differently is not to tell everyone, but rather just my family and those who went through my last loss with me.

If I were to get pregnant again, I would take more

time to focus for the positive things occurring in my pregnancy as well as eating better and exercising. I didn't feel like I did anything wrong, but I know I could do things better. I was also under a great deal of stress. Much of that stress wouldn't exist the next time, but I would ensure I had lower stress levels, especially since stress affects the baby, too. If you feel similarly, you can also take the time to focus on doing things even better for the next pregnancy. Eat right, exercise, and take time for yourself.

Bonding with your baby may be difficult. I had a conversation with Jason the other day about how he may feel during the next pregnancy. He told me that he wants to know when we can bond with the baby because he doesn't want to bond until he knows for sure the baby is going to survive. I told him there was no point in the pregnancy where we'll know for sure. We had a heartbeat and our baby was one of the 5% that died after we saw the heartbeat. I have read countless stories of babies dying the day before their due date and at birth. Jason was disappointed to hear that we'll never get to a point in the pregnancy where we can feel relaxed and certain of our destiny.

Despite the uncertainty, I believe it's best to try to bond with the new baby. I feel like the loss won't be any different because I will still be hopeful that the baby will live, so it's best to bond and nurture the baby from the moment we know we are pregnant. It will be difficult, but try to bond with your baby from the moment you know. It will be hard. If you fear bonding because of guilt, understand that nothing will replace the baby you lost. Each baby is an individual.

Asherman's Syndrome

"Asherman's Syndrome is an acquired uterine condition, characterized by the formation of adhesions (scar tissue) inside the uterus. It occurs when trauma to the endometrial lining triggers the normal wound-healing process, which causes the damaged areas to fuse together. Most commonly, intrauterine adhesions occur after a D&C (dilation and curettage) that was performed because of a missed or incomplete miscarriage, because of retained placenta, or pregnancy termination. Pregnancy-related D&Cs have been shown to account for 90% of Asherman's cases (see reference materials). Adhesions sometimes also occur following other pelvic surgeries such as cesarean section, surgery to remove fibroids, polyps, or to correct a congenital uterine defect (see reference materials).

The discovery of my Asherman's Syndrome was a fluke. After my D&C, the few periods I had were extremely painful. I often had to take Tylenol with Codeine for several days because the pain was so intense. These weren't cramps; it was a constant pain in the center of my uterus that wouldn't go away. I would bleed, then it would stop. I would bleed again, and it would stop. Unlike my previous periods, this blood was usually dark purple. I ignored the strange periods for several months and was just happy that I was ovulating regularly.

After my daughter's due date, I became "crazed." I desperately wanted a baby. I wanted to grow a baby inside me and I wanted to do it NOW! It couldn't come fast enough. I was still scared to attempt another pregnancy though. I began talking with Jason about getting fertility treatments again so we could start with all the proper monitoring and ensure I had hormonal supplementation from the very beginning. I didn't want to experience another miscarriage, and even though I was ovulating regularly, I wanted the benefit of monitoring my hormone levels so I had the best possibility for successful implantation.

Before I attempted another pregnancy, I wanted to make sure that my right ovary wasn't full of cysts. It was still hurting me from time to time, and the pain was beginning to get out of control. Years before, I had an ultrasound and was told there were over 50 cysts on the ovary and I should have it removed to prevent cancer. There was no way I would have an ovary removed, so I just lived with the pain. I called my doctor regarding the pain, and he set me up with an ultrasound of my ovaries.

The ultrasound went without a hitch, and it looked like my new-found ovulation was assisting with reducing the cysts in my ovaries because the ultrasound technician stated the ovaries looked good. With that out of the way, I scheduled an appointment with the reproductive endocrinologist. The first appointment revealed I couldn't attempt a pregnancy without having surgery. My reproductive endocrinologist had reviewed my recent ultrasound even though it wasn't related to any appointment I had with him. He told me my ovaries looked fine but there was something inside my uterine cavity. He showed me two white spots with black spots in between them inside my uterus.

As if all that happened with my loss wasn't enough, now it looked as if my loss had caused me more fertility issues. The pain I was having with my periods wasn't unwarranted. Apparently, I had a webbing of scar tissue in my uterus and if I got pregnant, I would either miscarry or I could tear my uterus apart. The doctor needed to fix what was wrong with my uterus.

The D&C from my loss caused damage inside my

uterus. My uterine walls lied together following the procedure. With the walls lying together, the cuts scarred together causing a web of scar tissue. Some doctors will place a balloon in the uterus to help prevent this from happening, but that wasn't the case for me. An easier way for me to understand what had happened was to imagine my uterine walls as being two pancakes with jelly spread in between them. The jelly represented my uterine lining, soft, thick, and ready to nourish a baby. If one tried to lift the top pancake, the jelly would keep the two pancakes together. If you were to look at the jelly, it's being pulled in both directions. This is the scar tissue and it would need to be cut.

I scheduled surgery to have the scars cut. It's a simple procedure and the doctor would place a balloon in my uterus to prevent the walls from scarring back together and also had me on estrogen therapy for a few weeks. Sounds easy enough, but I had to go through the same type of anesthesia again. I was worried. I made sure to discuss my concerns with the anesthesiologist, and I made sure that the same anesthesiologist at my D&C wasn't the anesthesiologist at this procedure.

The surgery went without a hitch, although I did have periods of having an extremely low heart rate again. I was monitored well, though, and the anesthesiologist was forthcoming with me about everything. The balloon in my uterus was extremely painful at first, but the doctor removed some of the saline and it felt much better. Still, I had tubes hanging out my vagina for a week, and when I sat down, I could feel the balloon in my uterus. The only other issue I had was that the surgery was almost exactly one year from my D&C surgery. My D&C was on April 16, 2010 and my uterine surgery was April 13, 2011. I was also in the exact same operating room and pre-op room.

It was surreal.

Following the procedure, I lost all desire to have another baby. Maybe that was God's way of slowing the drive down? I also stopped ovulating, which meant the only way to have a baby was to take fertility drugs. I was now barren. There is no explanation as to why ovulation ceased after the procedure. In many cases, women are more fertile following this type of procedure (see reference materials). I believe, once again, that my mind was made up and I no longer wanted to have a baby, so I forced myself to stop ovulating.

Blind D&C vs. Ultrasound with D&C

There are different ways for doctors to perform a D&C. I had a "blind" D&C. This means that the doctor performs the procedure without using an ultrasound machine to see what is happening inside the uterus. The doctor blindly scrapes away the lining of the uterus. This increases the chance that the doctor will perforate or "poke through" the uterine wall.

It's dangerous and can cause scarring (Asherman's Syndrome) or other complications such as incomplete removal of the products of conception. There is a 40% chance of an increase in scarring for secondary D&C's.

Another way to perform a D&C is with the use of an ultrasound. The doctor is guided through the uterus and scrapes only what is needed. It's more costly due to the use of extra technology, but definitely worth the extra money. There is still a risk of scarring, because any time you scrape the uterine lining you can cause scarring. The upside is that there is a reduced risk and less chance of a perforation. My goal is to have HMO's and other large insurance companies perform ultra-sound guided D&C's as these are safer.

Recovery

My daughter would be a little over a year old now. It's hard to believe I endured everything I have written in this book. This was truly the worst trauma I have ever experienced. I finally feel as if I am back to being me again. It took about nine months for me to start to feel "normal" again. I don't know if we can ever be exactly who we were before losing our babies, but I know that I feel a sense of peace around my experience. Everything in this book, including writing it, has helped me to feel that peace. I still think of my daughter often. Her announcement is taped to my bedroom mirror so I see her every day. I have learned that moving forward from grief is a life-long process and that the goal of moving forward is never about forgetting. I will always remember her and see her in my heart. This wasn't an easy road. Grief is painful, but it is possible to move forward . . . when one is ready.

I have talked with many women about their miscarriages over the last two years and the one question they have is, "When will I feel normal again?" The answer depends on the woman. I have witnessed some women who feel they have moved through their grief after only a week and other women who are still grieving decades after their loss. I wish there was an easy answer, but there's not.

At some point, you will most likely feel some sense of normalcy again. Some women describe feeling guilty when they start to feel "normal" as if that means they have somehow betrayed their lost one. When you begin to feel more at peace with your loss, remember it is okay to feel this and that you are not betraying your baby. Remember that moving forward and rejoining the living doesn't mean that you have forgotten the loss and its impact. You will have good days and bad days, and then one day you might come to realize that you are having more good days than bad. Only then will you know you are "normal" again.

Joey came into my office not too long ago and asked to look at the cover of this book again. He then said, "Mom, you are so brave to write about my baby sister." I started to cry. Then he said, "I wished we got to see what she looked like . . . but she was just a speck of blood." This was a very special moment for me. I learned my son still thinks of her. Even more importantly, I realized that my tears were no longer about my loss — they were about my recovery.

I am so sorry for your loss.

About the Author

I am first, and foremost, an ordinary woman — a woman of faith, family, and service. I hope that in sharing my experience many mothers, fathers, and siblings will find healing in their own journey.

I am a security manager, police officer, doula, former Marine, wife and mother. This tribute to my unborn daughter, Ruby Josephine, now propels me to the rank of author. This is a gift my daughter has given me.

For more information about me and the creation of this book and my blog, please visit the book's website at www.allthatisseenandunseen.com. Join me on Facebook at this book's fan page and reach out to others who understand. In this forum you will find strength but also be welcomed to lend your own, special wisdom.

Thank you for sharing my journey.

Elizabeth

Appendix

Ruby's Statistics

Ovulation – 2/28/10

Positive Pregnancy Test – 3/17/10

BETA HCG – 18 days past ovulation = 416
Progesterone – 18 days past ovulation = 11.6

BETA HCG – 20 days past ovulation = 918
Progesterone – 20 days past ovulation = 7.4

BETA HCG – 22 days past ovulation = 1751

BETA HCG – 45 days past ovulation = 7387

U/S 5w4d – 1 gestational sac @ 5mm
U/S 6w1d – 1 gestational sac, yolk sac, and fetal pole
w/possible heartbeat!
U/S 7w0d – 1 baby with heartbeat!
U/S 8w3d – No heartbeat 4/14/10

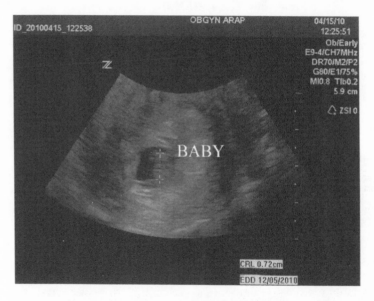

This is one of the only pictures I have of Ruby.

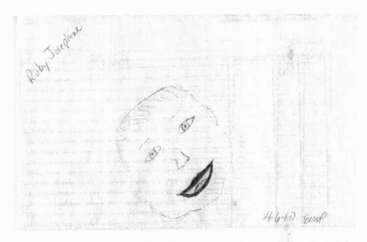

Picture I drew of my daughter while I was at work. This
was the day I named my daughter officially.

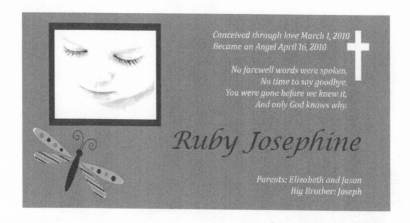

Conceived through love March 1, 2010
Became an Angel April 16, 2010

No farewell words were spoken,
No time to say goodbye,
You were gone before we knew it,
And only God knows why.

Ruby Josephine

Parents: Elizabeth and Jason
Big Brother: Joseph

Ruby's Announcement

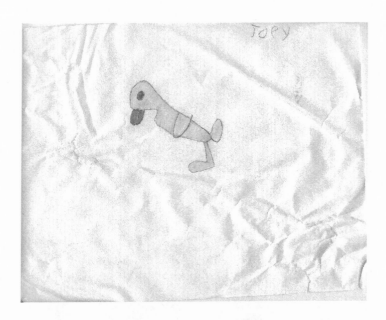

Art Joey drew for Ruby. He wanted this buried with her.

Photo provided by Tiffany Stull www.allisonphotography.com

My husband and I after he pinned on my badge.

Books:

Miscarriage: Women Sharing from the Heart by Marie Allen and Shelly Marks

Miscarriage: Women's Experiences and Needs by Christine Moulder (Out of Print)

Pregnancy After a Loss: A Guide to Pregnancy After a Miscarriage, Stillbirth, or Infant Death by Carol Cirulli Lanham

Empty Cradle, Broken Heart: Surviving the Death of Your Baby by Deborah L. Davis

A Silent Sorrow: Pregnancy Loss - Guidance and Support for You and Your Family by Ingrid Kohn and Perry-Lynn Moffitt

Gone Too Soon: The Life and Loss of Infants and Unborn Children by Sherri Devashrayee Wittwer

Books for Children:

Something Happened: A book for children and parents who have experienced pregnancy loss by Cathy Blanford and Phyllis Childers

We Were Gonna Have a Baby, But We Had an Angel Instead by Pat Schwiebert and Taylor Bills

Someone Came Before You by Pat Schwiebert

Support Groups:

Mommies Enduring Neonatal Death, (www.MEND.org)
Rowan Tree Foundation, (www.rowantreefoundation.org)
A Walk to Remember (www.walktoremember.org)
Asherman's Syndrome, (www.ashermans.org)
Polycystic Ovarian Syndrome Support Group, (www.soulcysters.net)
In Denver – Shadia Duske, (www.psychotherapy-healing.com/GROUPS.html)

Online Resources:

Now I Lay Me Down To Sleep (www.nilmdts.org)

Mother's Milk Bank of Denver,
(www.milkbankcolorado.org)

My Forever Child – Keepsakes and Jewelry for Remembrance, Healing, and Hope
(www.myforeverchild.com)

Reference Material:

Grief and depression after miscarriage: their separation, antecedents, and course, M Beutel, R Deckardt, M von Rad and H Weiner; Psychosomatic Medicine, Vol 57, Issue 6 517-526, Copyright © 1995 by American Psychosomatic Society, accessed from http://www.psychosomaticmedicine.org/content/57/6/51 7.short on 1/11/12.

After a Miscarriage: Physical Recovery; accessed from http://www.americanpregnancy.org/pregnancyloss/mcp hysicalrecovery.html on 1/11/12

Intra-uterine adhesions: an updated appraisal. Schenker JG, Margalioth EJ. Fertility Sterility 1982; 37:593-610)

www.ashermans.org; accessed 1/11/12

The effectiveness of hysteroscopy in improving pregnancy rates in subfertile women without other gynaecological symptoms: a systematic review; accessed from http://www.ncbi.nlm.nih.gov/pubmed/19744944 on 1/11/12).

Reference Material Continued:

Cytotec; accessed from
http://www.fda.gov/medwatch/safety/2000/cytote.htm
on 1/11/12 and
http://www.cytoteccase.com/FDA%20Safety%20Alert.
htm on 1/11/12